LAYMAN'S LIBRARY OF CHRISTIAN DOCTRINE

Life in the Spirit
EARL C. DAVIS

BROADMAN PRESS
Nashville, Tennessee

To four churches who demonstrate life in the Spirit:

Ekron Baptist Church, Ekron, Kentucky

First Baptist Church, Marianna, Florida

First Baptist Church, Dalton, Georgia

First Baptist Church, Memphis, Tennessee

© Copyright 1986 • Broadman Press

All rights reserved

4216-41

ISBN: 0-8054-1641-2

Dewey Decimal Classification: 230

Subject Heading: THEOLOGY

Library of Congress Catalog Card Number: 86-13676

Printed in the United States of America

Library of Congress Cataloging-in-Publication Data

Davis, Earl C.
  Life in the Spirit.

  (Layman's library of Christian doctrine ; 11)
  Includes index.
  1. Spiritual life—Baptist authors.   I. Title.
II. Series.
BV4501.2.D383   1986   248.4′86132   86-13676
ISBN 0-8054-1641-2

Foreword

The *Layman's Library of Christian Doctrine* in sixteen volumes covers the major doctrines of the Christian faith.

To meet the needs of the lay reader, the *Library* is written in a popular style. Headings are used in each volume to help the reader understand which part of the doctrine is being dealt with. Technical terms, if necessary to the discussion, will be clearly defined.

The need for this series is evident. Christians need to have a theology of their own, not one handed to them by someone else. The *Library* is written to help readers evaluate and form their own beliefs based on the Bible and on clear and persuasive statements of historic Christian positions. The aim of the series is to help laymen hammer out their own personal theology.

The books range in size from 140 pages to 168 pages. Each volume deals with a major part of Christian doctrine. Although some overlap is unavoidable, each volume will stand on its own. A set of the sixteen-volume series will give a person a complete look at the major doctrines of the Christian church.

Each volume is personalized by its author. The author will show the vitality of Christian doctrines and their meaning for everyday life. Strong and fresh illustrations will hold the interest of the reader. At times the personal faith of the authors will be seen in illustrations from their own Christian pilgrimage.

Not all laymen are aware they are theologians. Many may believe they known nothing of theology. However, every person believes something. This series helps the layman to understand what he believes and to be able to be "prepared to make a defense to anyone who calls him to account for the hope that is in him" (1 Pet. 3:15, RSV).

Preface

As the promises of Jesus reveal, and the experience of the early church and modern Christians confirm, the life in the Spirit is dynamic, not static. It is an experience first, then, in a secondary sense, it is doctrinal.

The purpose of this book is not so much to develop a statement of the doctrine of the Holy Spirit, or to do the exegetical spadework of such a study, but rather to explore the experienced life in the Spirit. A further purpose is to lead you and me to examine the closeness of our daily Christian life to that which the Scripture says is the "life in the Spirit."

My prayer is that, as you join me in this pilgrimage to understand the dynamics of this life in the Spirit, it might be a personal time of renewal. I cannot express this hope more aptly than in the words of William Barclay in his foreword to his fine study on the Holy Spirit, *The Promise of the Spirit*.

> I can only say that the study of the teaching of the New Testament about the Holy Spirit has been for me personally a humiliating, a challenging, and a comforting experience—humiliating, because it has been driven home upon me how far short I have come of experiencing the splendour of life in the Spirit; challenging, because I have dimly glimpsed heights of Christian experience which may yet be reached; comforting, because I never before realized the reservoir of divine power which is available to the man who will commit his life to Jesus Christ."[1]

Note

1. William Barclay, *The Promise of the Spirit* (Philadelphia: The Westminster Press, 1960), pp. 9-10.

Contents

1. The Decision: Who Controls My Life? 7

2. The Description: What Does Life in the Spirit
   Look Like? 26

3. The Dynamic: What Decides the Shape
   of My Spiritual Life? 43

4. The Devotion: Do I Practice the Presence? 56

5. The Deeper Life: How Can I Deepen My Devotional
   Life 73

6. The Development: Do I have Spiritual Gifts
   and Spiritual Fruit? 90

7. The Direction: When Is the Church Really
   the Church? 110

8. The Defiant Life: Is There Victory Over
   the Devil? 122

9. The Destiny: Tell Me Again About the Promised
   Victory 130

   Bibliography 138

   Scripture Index 138

Contents

1. ...You Can Live As ... Life ....

2. The Everyone's Mailbox Insurance Salesman
Book 28

3. "God Grant Me a Place to die for Stuff"
at My Spiritual Job 28

4. The Reason to Do It Just for the Reaction 20

5. The Person Who Have Told Painted My... Devotions
.... 73

6. The ... Anagrams: They Have Solved All the
no against losing 90

7. The Direction When It Is Completely ...
the Opening 110

8. Ask ... Sin ... to Culture Variety Off ...
the Perfect 122

9. ... of Person Still the Again about the ... the seen
Moral 130

Bibliography 138

Scripture Index (topics) 135

1

The Decision
Who Controls My Life?

May I Ask You a Question?

Do you feel *you* are adequately experiencing the presence and power of the Holy Spirit? This volume in the Layman's Library of Christian Doctrine deals with our life in the Holy Spirit. *The Holy Spirit,* volume 10, by Wayne Ward deals primarily with the biblical material in an exegetical and doctrinal fashion; my intention here is to focus upon the *experience* of life in the Spirit. Long before the Holy Spirit was a doctrinal theme, He was an experienced fact, a person, to the Christian community. That is why there is such variety, in the midst of a basic unity, in the writings of the New Testament. Do you feel *you* are adequately experiencing the power and the presence of the Holy Spirit?

Your response may be, "I don't quite know what you're talking about." Most Christians do not reflect upon the reality of the Holy Spirit between Sundays. And, in many churches, there is little emphasis on either the doctrine or experience of the Spirit beyond the reciting of creeds. Without guidance, church members may have a vague and confused grasp of the Spirit. As Harry Emerson Fosdick once said, "The idea of God in three persons is difficult enough without compounding the difficulty by calling one of them a 'Ghost.'" Dr. E. Y. Mullins said, "It's a strange and significant fact that Christians for nearly two thousand years have so generally neglected the New Testament teaching concerning the Holy Spirit." It does, indeed, seem as if the sin of the Old Testament was the rejection of God the Father; the sin of the New Testament period was the rejection of God the Son; and now, in our time, the sin is that of rejecting God the Holy Spirit.

Another response to my question, "Do you feel *you* are adequately

7

experiencing the presence and power of the Holy Spirit?" may be to say—"If you're from one of those charismatic groups, count me out!" What a sad commentary on our experience of the Spirit! There is so much more to the rich life in the Spirit than those things which many of us feel are misunderstandings and excesses in the areas of spiritual gifts. Yet you may have to deal with your feelings about the phenomenon of "tongues," faith healing, and other characteristics of the "charismatic" movement before you can comfortably explore the life in the Spirit.

To my question whether you are experiencing the full and transforming presence of the Spirit, some folks answer by replying, "I'm about worn out with church work—if you have any more power for me, let's hear about it!" Unfortunately, while the early Christians' experience of the Spirit was real, too often our only spiritual reality is that of the church and its institutional demands upon us. The more we work, the less joy and spiritual power we seem to have.

Not long ago I bought a bicycle. A shiny, sleek, brand-new, dark green bike. I was well pleased with my purchase and began to ride it with great enthusiasm. Now, part of the reason I took up cycling was the glowing recommendation from a friend who said he was riding seven miles each morning before breakfast. And so I set out on my morning rides with a sporty Scottish cap and a cyclometer (that's a fancy word which means a bicycle speedometer) to measure how far I rode. Three miles. In thirty minutes? Not being a cyclist, I just grumbled and kept on going. The next day I nearly pedaled myself to death and collected only five miles or so. After a couple of days, my wife suggested we check the cyclometer by the car speedometer. To my dismay, I found I was pedaling three miles for every one mile being registered! The cyclometer had not been set correctly. The harder I worked, the behinder I got! I see people in our churches who feel this way about their spiritual life. Could it be that we have forgotten a vital component of our spiritual life—the Holy Spirit?

"Do you feel *you* are adequately experiencing the presence and power of the Holy Spirit?" Most Christians do not reflect upon the matter. Sometimes only a crisis will cause us to wonder if our experience is all there is to the life in the Spirit. H. Wheeler Robinson, a great English Baptist scholar of the first half of this century, penned one of the finest studies of the Christian experience of the Holy Spirit. In *The Christian Experience of the Holy Spirit,* he tells how he came to write on the subject. During a serious illness, be began to wonder why the truths of the Christian faith which he had so long preached failed to give him the personal strength he needed in such a crisis. The truths were true, but they seemed to lack vitality. The realization of the comfort and power of his faith seemed to require great effort on his part, which was beyond him. It was as if the faith was a great balloon, with ample power to lift, if only he had the strength to grasp the rope which trailed down from the balloon! A study of his own faith led him to see a lack in his realization of the power and presence of the Holy Spirit in the believer's life.[1] That incident is a parable of the spiritual life of so many of us.

"Do you feel *you* are adequately experiencing the presence and power of the Holy Spirit?" While Christians seem to give little thought to the place of the Holy Spirit, many Christians are genuinely hungry for something more, something deeper in their spiritual pilgrimages. The other day I was out riding—with the cyclometer properly set—and listening to a talk show on a tiny radio. In less than an hour on that program I heard views on faith healing, speaking in "tongues," and the phenomenal rise of both authentic and inauthentic media evangelists. The charismatic movement, which seemed to crest in the seventies, is still very much on the religious scene. Emphasis on faith healing seems to be intensifying. Indeed, this is an age of much ado about religion, and I feel that the packaging of religion in partnership with politics, authority, self-help, and patriotism is an expression of spiritual hunger for a deeper and more genuine experience.

Christians are seeking the reality of the presence of the Holy Spirit. We have been taught all our religious lives that, at our conversion, the Holy Spirit comes to dwell within us. I believe every Christian is *indwelt* by the Holy Spirit, but not every Christian experiences the *reality* of the presence of the Holy Spirit.

Testimonies to the Rich Life in the Spirit

In our study of life in the Spirit, the testimonies of Christians who experienced the reality of the presence and power of the Holy Spirit can be helpful. I have selected these individuals not necessarily because they are spiritual giants but because their names are familiar to most of us. Equally valid testimonies could be drawn from the fellowship of your church and mine.

David Brainerd

David Brainerd (1718-1747) poured out his life serving Christ as a missionary to the New England Indians. He was dead at twenty-nine after five years' work. John Wesley is said to have directed that all his "Methodist" preachers carefully read the life of Brainerd: "Let us be followers of him, as he was of Christ, in absolute self-devotion, in total deafness to the world and in fervent love to God and man." Brainerd's total harvest for Jesus was eighty-five Indians. In his diary, published after his death by the great New England minister, Johnathan Edwards, in whose home Brainerd died, the entry for April 27, 1742 reads:

> I arose and retired early for secret devotions; and in prayer, God was pleased to pour such ineffable comforts into my soul, that I could do nothing for some time but say over and over, "O My sweet Saviour! whom have I in Heaven but thee? and there is none upon earth that I desire beside thee." If I had a thousand lives, my soul would gladly have laid them all down at once, to have been with Christ. My soul never enjoyed so much of heaven before; it was the most refined and most spiritual season of communion with God I ever yet felt.[2]

Edwards, commenting on Brainerd's diary, said

> His religion apparently greatly differed from that of many high pretenders of religion, who are frequently actuated by vehement emotions of mind, and are carried on in a course of sudden and strong impressions, and supposed high illuminations and immediate discoveries . . . if we look through the whole series of his experience, from his conversation to his death, we shall find none of this kind—no imaginary sight of Christ hanging on the cross with his blood streaming from his wounds; or with a countenance smiling on him; or arms open to embrace him; no sight of the book of life opened, with his name written in it; no hearing God or Christ speaking to him; nor any sudden suggestions of words or sentences, either of Scripture or any other. . . . Nor do I find any one instance in all the records which he has left on his own life, from beginning to end, of joy excited from a supposed immediate witness of the Spirit; or inward immediate suggestion, that his state was surely good. But the way in which he satisfied of his own good estate, even to the entire abolishing of fear, was *by feeling within himself the lively actings of a holy temper* and heavenly disposition, the vigorous exercises of that divine "love which casteth out fear."[3]

Andrew Murray

Andrew Murray (1828-1917) gave his life as a minister in South Africa. Upon Murray's death at eighty-nine, his friends erected a beautiful marble statue of him in front of his old church. Esteem for him was so great that drunks staggering home feared to pass that way because "the old minister will see us!" So holy had been his life among them, they trembled to pass by even his image in stone. Amy Carmichael, herself a model of the Spirit-filled life, tells in one of her books of meeting Murray and boarding at the same house. Something painful happened to Murray, and this is how he met it:

> He was quiet for a while with his Lord, then he wrote these words for himself:
> First, he brought me here, it is by His will I am in this strait place: in that fact I will rest.
> Next, He will keep me here in His love, and give me grace to behave as His child.
> Then, He will make the trial a blessing, teaching me the lessons He intends me to learn, and working in me the grace He means to bestow.
> Last, in His good time He can bring me out again—how and when He knows.
> Let me say I am here,
> (1) By God's appointment,
> (2) In His keeping,
> (3) Under His training,
> (4) For His time.[4]

That kind of patient submission to the will of God, that kind of testimony among those to whom he ministered, come from the indwelling Spirit, not from the natural human heart.

Adoniram Judson Gordon

Adoniram Judson Gordon (1836-1895) was an outstanding pastor whose life was transformed by a dream. In the dream he was standing before his congregation about to begin the sermon when a stranger entered the church. He came down the aisle, took a seat, and fixed his attention on the preacher. The preacher could not keep his eyes off the stranger; it was as if the man looked right into his soul. At the close of the service, the stranger slipped out before the minister could reach him. Finding the parishioner by whom the stranger sat, the minister asked if he knew the man. The reply was, "Why, do you not know that man? It was Jesus of Nazareth." At the pastor's disappointment, the man said, "Oh, do not be troubled. He has been here today and no doubt he will come again."[5] The truth spoken by the man in the dream—"Here today and to come again"—brought to glorious light for Gordon the reality of the presence of the Holy Spirit of Jesus, as well as the assurance and reality of the second coming. His ministry was never the same.

David Livingstone

Surely nothing but the Spirit of the exalted Christ could be the basis for the life of David Livingstone (1841-1873). He spent thirty years as a missionary in Africa. He traveled 29,000 miles, and everywhere he went he took the gospel of Christ. As one biographer put it, "It was the highest tribute that the slave-traders in the Zambesi district paid to his character when for their own vile ends they told the people that they were the children of Livingstone. . . . The noble conduct of the band that for eight months carried his remains toward the coast was a crowning proof of the love he inspired."[6]

During a visit to Livingstone's hometown of Blantyre in Scotland, I saw his battered diary with its entry for January 14, 1856, on the night before going into unfriendly and very dangerous new territory:

Evening.—Felt much turmoil of spirit in view of having all my plans for the welfare of this great region and teeming population knocked on the head by savages to-morrow. But I read that Jesus came and said, "All power is given unto me in heaven and in earth. Go ye therefore, and teach all nations—and lo, *I am with you alway, even unto the end of the world*" [emphasis Livingstone's]. It is the word of a gentleman of the most sacred and strictest honor, and there is an end on't. I will not cross furtively by night as I intended. It would appear as flight, and should such a man as I flee?[7]

The entry in Livingstone's diary for his fifty-ninth birthday, March 19, 1872, reads: "My Jesus, my King, my Life, my All; I again dedicate my whole self to Thee."[8] About a year later, he was found in death kneeling beside his bed, as in prayer.

Dietrich Bonhoeffer

Dietrich Bonhoeffer (1906-1945) is known to Christians everywhere as a martyr to the Christian faith who perished during the Hitler nightmare. A German theologian, he opposed Hitler openly as early as 1933 and had to leave Germany that year to teach and preach in England. Returning in 1935, he demonstrated with his life the central theme of his most famous book, *The Cost of Discipleship*—that when Christ calls a man, he bids him come and die. Bonhoeffer clearly realized that *"one's own will must always be abandoned to the divine will, that one's own will must be given up, if the divine will is to be manifested"* [emphasis mine].[9]

Bonhoeffer worked with the Confessional Church and the political underground movement during the war, becoming involved in the attempts on Hitler's life. In 1943 he was arrested by the Gestapo. The last note from Bonhoeffer while in Tegel prison, smuggled out on August 21, 1944, deals with his morning meditation:

> Once again I have taken up the *Losungen* [the Bible passages for the day] and meditated on them. *The key to everything is the "in him"*. All that we may rightly expect from God, and ask him for, is to be found in Jesus Christ. If we are to learn what God promises, and what he fulfills, we must persevere it in quiet meditation on the life, sayings, deeds, sufferings, and death of Jesus. It is certain that we may always live close to God and in the light of his presence, and that such living is an entirely new life for us; that nothing is then impossible for us, because all things are possible with God; that no earthly power can touch us without his will, and that danger and distress can only drive us closer to him.[10]

An English officer who was also imprisoned in Buchenwald during Bonhoeffer's last days there described him: "Bonhoeffer was different; just quite calm and normal, seemingly perfectly at his ease . . . his soul really shone in the dark desperation of our prison. . . . He was one of the very few men I have ever met to whom his God was real, and ever close to him."[11]

On April 9, 1945, only three weeks before Hitler committed suicide and a few days before the Allies liberated the prison camp at Flossenburg where Bonhoeffer had been taken, Bonhoeffer and several other prisoners were taken at dawn to a place of execution in a wooded glen and there hanged. The prison doctor wrote years later of seeing Bonhoeffer an hour or so before his death: "Through the half-open door of a room in one of the huts I saw Pastor Bonhoeffer, still in his prison clothes, kneeling in fervent prayer to the Lord his God. The devotion and evident conviction of being heard that I saw in the prayer of this intensely captivating man, moved me to the depths."[12]

Each of the persons whose experience of life in the Spirit have been briefly outlined *felt a presence and a power which was beyond man; a presence which they firmly believed to be that of God's Holy Spirit.* The experience is not always stated in the same terms, but it is always the one and same Spirit guiding, comforting, encouraging, whether felt as the pressure of God the Father or the personality of Jesus the Son. Was their experience of the Spirit in keeping with that which *you* have experienced? Is it true to the Bible? What did Jesus promise His followers?

The Promise of Jesus

We must begin by asking ourselves if our experience of the presence of the Holy Spirit rings true to the promises Jesus made in John 14 and 16. At the Last Supper account in John 14, Jesus sought to comfort His disciples who were filled with apprehension and fear as they sensed impending doom.

The familiar passage begins with the words about the Father's house: "Let not your heart by troubled" (v. 1) and goes on to say that when He leaves, the Father will send another "Comforter" (v. 16), a Paraclete; one who will be alongside the believer.

The Paraclete

What is meant by the *Paraclete?* This word is found only in the writings of John in the New Testament. One way this term is used is that of an advocate, or defense attorney. We can point to the way the Holy Spirit defended the disciples when they were on trial (Matt. 10:20), but in John's Gospel the Paraclete is more of a prosecuting attorney, convicting the world. Paraclete can also mean "a spokesman," a mediator, or a helper. This word is also related to the Greek word for *comfort* and has to do with encouraging.

We can put the statements about the *Paraclete* in John 14—16 into four categories: the Paraclete's coming, His identification, His relationship to the disciples, and His relationship to the world.[13]

The Paraclete would come when Jesus departed (15:26; 16:7-8,13),

He would come from the Father (15:26), the Father would give the Paraclete at Jesus' request (14:16), He would be sent in Jesus' name (14:26), and Jesus would send the Paraclete when He left (15:26; 16:7).

The Paraclete is identified in Greek as "another [Paraclete]" (14:16), He is the "Spirit of truth" (14:17; 15:26; 16:13), and He is the Holy Spirit (14:26, RSV).

In terms of the relationship of the Paraclete to the disciples, they would recognize Him. He would be with them and remain with them (14:17). He would teach them (v. 26), guide them in the way of the truth (16:13), take what belonged to Jesus and declare it to the disciples, glorify Jesus (v. 14), bear witness on Jesus' behalf—as must the disciples (15:26-27). He would remind the disciples of all Jesus told them (14:26) and speak only what He heard (16:13).

The Paraclete and the World

The relationship of the Paraclete to the world includes the inability of the world to see, recognize, or accept Him (14:17); He bears witness to Jesus in the midst of the world's hatred for the followers of Jesus (15:26); and He will prove the world wrong about sin, justice, and judgment (16:8-11).

These promises concerning the Paraclete tell us that He comes from the Father, that He is the Holy Spirit, that He will dwell within the disciples of Jesus and teach, guide, and remind them of Jesus and His truth, and that He will bear witness to the world, convicting, and reproving a wicked world.

Now, unless these promises are limited to the first circle of disciples, you and I can expect to experience the same reality of the Spirit. Does your experience of the Holy Spirit ring true to the promises of Jesus?

The Experience of the Early Church
The Book of Acts

What is the picture of the church in the Book of Acts with regard to the Holy Spirit? Was the church dominated by its organizations or programs or pastors or deacons? Or was it rather controlled by the reality of the Spirit? A casual reading of Acts will show how real and vital the Spirit was to the church.

Power came with the coming of the Spirit at Pentecost. The disciples were filled with the Spirit; and through the filling of the Spirit, Peter withstood the priests. As the young church prayed, the members were filled with the Spirit, the meeting place was shaken, and they went forth to witness boldly.

Deceiving the church was seen to be a sin against the Holy Spirit. The first deacons were men filled with the Spirit, and Stephen was full of the Spirit as he died under a rain of stones. The churches found comfort in the Holy Spirit and grew, even under persecution. The Spirit caught Philip away after he baptized the Ethiopian eunuch. Ananias announced that God had sent him to the converted Saul that Saul's sight might be restored and that he might be filled with the Holy Spirit.

The Spirit interpreted Peter's rooftop vision at Joppa and sent Peter to Cornelius. While Peter preached to the Gentiles, the Holy Spirit fell on them, astonishing the Jewish Christians with Peter, and leading to water baptism. Peter emphasized the role of the Spirit in reporting this experience to the church in Jerusalem.

Barnabas, filled with the Spirit, was sent to the church at Antioch; Agabus, by the Spirit, prophesied a famine; and the Holy Spirit told the church in Antioch to set Paul and Barnabas apart for missionary service.

Through the power or the Spirit, Paul struck blind the sorcerer Elymas. At the Jerusalem conference to discuss requirements to be placed on Paul's Gentile converts, it "seemed good to the Holy Spirit and to us to lay upon you no greater burden than these necessary things" (Acts 15:28, RSV). The Holy Spirit directed the route of the second missionary journey and witnessed in every city concerning Paul's fate awaiting him at Jerusalem.

A clear current of the reality of the Holy Spirit and an expectancy of His guidance runs through the Book of Acts. The indwelling of the Spirit was and is a natural part of the Christian experience. Power accompanied this indwelling presence, a power both spiritual (as the church prayed, and as the disciples and deacons preached) and physical (the shaking of the building). The Spirit was a constant presence who brought comfort in difficult situations, gave an understanding of God's will, and guided, instructed, and warned the church.

Paul's Letters

A study of Paul's letters reveals the same direction and control of the Holy Spirit over the individual Christian and the church in general. The

Holy Spirit leads Christians, makes intercession for the saints, helps our infirmities, and sanctifies believers. The Spirit can be grieved and quenched. He searches the Christians' hearts and gives spiritual gifts. The Spirit dwells in believers, washes and justifies Christians, and gives liberty. We are temples of the Spirit and are being changed into the image of our Lord by the Spirit.

The Rest of the New Testament

Moving beyond the earliest descriptions of life in the Spirit in the Book of Acts and Paul's earlier letters, we find confirmation of the emphases already mentioned. Through the eternal Spirit, Christ offered Himself for our sins (Heb. 9:14). The close relationship of Christ and the Spirit seems to overlap in the Book of Revelation as the Spirit is seen as the exalted Christ (compare Rev. 2:1,7-8,11).

The Spirit is closely tied to salvation: God has saved us by the renewing of the Spirit (Titus 3:5), we are sanctified by the Spirit (1 Pet. 1:2), and "we know that [God] abideth in us, by the Spirit which he hath given us" (1 John 3:24). One of the most dreadful passages on punishment is the statement in Hebrews 10:29 in its reference to the person who has "trodden under foot the Son of God, . . . and hath done despite unto the Spirit of grace."

Teaching is stressed as a continuing work of the Spirit. He rebukes, warns, and interprets the Old Testament (Heb. 3:7; 9:8; 10:15; Rev. 14:13; 1 Pet. 1:11). The Spirit verifies and validates the gospel by enabling us to guard the treasure entrusted to us (2 Tim. 1:14), by the giving of special spiritual gifts, and by testing the spirits (1 John 4:1-6). The Spirit also gives visions to the Christian community (Rev. 1:10; 4:2; 17:3; 21:10).

We must ask ourselves whether our experience as individual Christians and as part of a church is like that described above. If not, why not?

The Relationship of the Holy Spirit to Jesus

What is the relationship of the Holy Spirit to Jesus of Nazareth? Some New Testament passages speak of the Holy Spirit as another Advocate, a separate person from Jesus (see John 14:16-18,26; 15:26; 16:7,13-15). Other passages seem to identify Jesus with the Holy Spirit (see John 14:18; 16:16; Rom. 8:9-11; 1 Cor. 6:17; 12:4-6; Gal. 2:20; Col. 1:27).

How shall we understand the mystery of the relationship between Jesus and the Spirit?

Jesus and the Holy Spirit

Matthew, Mark, Luke, and John tell of the descent of the Holy Spirit upon Jesus at His baptism. John the Baptist testified, "I saw the Spirit descending from heaven like a dove, and it abode upon him" (John 1:32). The Baptist also said, "I knew him not: but he that sent me to baptize with water, the same said unto me, upon whom thou shalt see the Spirit descending, and remaining on him, the same is he which baptizeth with the Holy Ghost" (v. 33). At least two things are shown in this passage.

The Holy Spirit remained in Jesus.—In the Old Testament, the Holy Spirit came upon persons for a specific task. Later, He might leave the person. However the Holy Spirit came upon Jesus and took up residence in Him. This was the beginning of a new day. From the time of Jesus until now, the Holy Spirit enters believers and remains with them.

The Holy Spirit is separate from Jesus.—Here we deal with mystery—the mystery of the Trinity. It is the mystery of how Jesus and the Holy Spirit can be the same yet different. They are the same in the sense they are God. They are different in the way Christians experience them.

Jesus and the Spirit as Experienced in the Early Church

God revealed Himself as Father, Son, and Holy Spirit. God as Father is seen in the Old Testament as He created, called, guided, judged, and rescued the chosen people. Jesus' life and teachings further clarified the character of God the Father. The personality of Jesus is made clear to us through the Gospels. The early church experienced the personality of the Holy Spirit to be the character of Jesus. This means they experienced the Holy Spirit as the invisible yet ever-present Jesus. The Holy Spirit reminded the early Christians of Jesus.

God is One.—The early Christians strongly affirmed that God is one, not many. They worshiped only God. Yet, as the disciples walked and talked with Jesus, as they saw the crucifixion and the resurrection, they became convinced that *Jesus was God!* Not another god, but another *expression* of the one God.

Jesus and the Spirit were closely identified.—After Pentecost and the ascension of Jesus, in accord with Jesus' promises, the presence of the Spirit of God filled the lives of the disciples and the church as whole. In fact, the Spirit the early Christians came to know in their lives—guiding, comforting, correcting, fellowshipping—was the same they had experienced when Jesus was with them on earth.

John's Gospel speaks of Jesus' leaving and sending *another* Advocate, indicating that the Holy Spirit has the character and qualities of Jesus. Luke said that the Holy Spirit would guide the persecuted disciples in what they would say when arrested (12:12). In another discussion, Luke quoted Jesus as saying He, Himself, would give disciples answers (21:12-15).

In Peter's vision on the rooftop in Joppa, Peter understood the voice at first to be that of the Lord, while a few minutes later the Spirit spoke (Acts 10:14-19).

Paul's plans to evangelize Asia Minor were first changed by the Holy Spirit (Acts 16:6), then changed again shortly after by the Spirit of Jesus (v. 7). In the beautiful eighth chapter of Romans, Paul, in the space of three verses, referred to the Holy Spirit as "the Spirit," "Spirit of God," "Spirit of Christ," "Christ," and "Spirit of him who raised up Jesus from the dead" (Rom. 8:9-11).

After Jesus' ascension, His followers felt the presence and leadership of the Holy Spirit. They realized that the Spirit was like Jesus of Nazareth. This closeness of the Spirit to Jesus can be seen in three accounts of Paul's conversion. In each passage, Paul related the question of Christ: "Saul, Saul, why persecutest thou me?" (Acts 9:4; 22:7; 26:14). Saul's answer, "Who art Thou, Lord?" received the astonishing answer: "I am Jesus [of Nazareth (22:8)] whom thou persecutest" (9:5; 26:15). Saul had never seen or met Jesus in the flesh, as far as we know, so what is meant here? Simply this, that the Holy Spirit, which filled the individual Christians and the Church as a whole and directed and empowered it, was so identified with their experience of the earthly Jesus that to persecute those filled with the Spirit was to persecute Jesus Himself.

The early Christians thought of the Spirit in rather concrete terms. He was no "Ghost." Instead, the Spirit was like a Friend who walked among them, smiled, helped, and healed them. As James Denny put it graphically: "No apostle, no New Testament writer, ever *remembered* Jesus"[14] because He was always near. Therefore, I understand the nature and work of the Holy Spirit better if I simply think of Him as the invisible yet ever-present Jesus.

Conclusion.—When we read John's account of the Last Supper conversation, the Book of Acts, and the accounts of Paul's work, we may feel the difference between these two persons of the Trinity (Son and Spirit) is not clear. That is because the New Testament is the white-hot testimony of those who were thrilled and overwhelmed by the presence and influence of Jesus. The writers were telling of their life-changing experiences with Jesus; they were not trying to present a carefully pondered theological statement of the Trinity. That task was carried out later by the church councils who used the Bible as the basis for their theological statements.

Jesus and the Spirit are separate and different persons of the Trinity. We are correct in singing, "God in three persons, blessed Trinity." The one God has revealed Himself to us as Father, Son, and Holy Spirit. As Frank Stagg has said, "The Holy Spirit, then, is not a third god nor one third of God. The Holy Spirit is God himself in his nearness and power, anytime and anywhere, the same divine presence as we know in the word made flesh, Immanuel."[15]

The Holy Spirit: Mere Presence or Actual Control?

Many Christians are confused about some of the terms used to speak of the relationship between Christians and the Holy Spirit. We speak of the gift of the Holy Spirit, the coming of the Spirit into believers' lives, being filled with the Spirit, and the control of the Spirit over our lives. A difference does exist between the *presence* of the Holy Spirit in a believer's life, and the *control* of that same life by the Holy Spirit.

The Old Testament Background

The primary background of the New Testament is the Old Testament. Not everyone in the Old Testament experienced the presence of the Spirit of God. In an unpredictable fashion, the Spirit fell upon whomever He wished. The coming of the Spirit upon people was not the result of their request or voluntary choice. People previously unknown were suddenly thrust into leadership positions simply because they had the presence of the Spirit—as we see in the stories of Deborah, Gideon, Jepthah, and David.

In the Old Testament, the presence of the Spirit was also, in general, a temporary experience. Just as persons did not know when the Spirit was going to come upon them, neither did they know when the Spirit might leave. In 1 Samuel we read that the Spirit of the Lord departed from Saul and came upon David. The transient nature of the Spirit, or at least David's fear of His leaving, is seen in Psalm 51: "and take not thy holy Spirit from me" (v. 11).

The New Testament Understanding: Abiding Presence

In the New Testament, the experience of receiving the gift of the Spirit, of having the presence of the Spirit—different ways of expressing the same reality—is the birthright and privilege of every believer. In contrast to the Old Testament experience, the New Testament emphasis is on the permanent presence of the Spirit in the believer. In John 14 we have the promise of Jesus: "And I will pray the Father, and he shall give you another Comforter, that he may abide with you for ever; (v. 16). And again in verse 17: "ye know him [the Comforter]; because he dwelleth with you, and shall be in you."

This emphasis on the constant and abiding presence is further seen in the preaching of Peter at Pentecost: "Repent, and be baptized every one of you in the name of Jesus Christ for the remission of sin, and ye shall receive the gift of the Holy [Spirit]. For the promise is unto you, and to your children, and to all that are afar off" (Acts 2:38-39). This same theme of the abiding presence, the gift of the Spirit, is seen in account after account of believers being given the Holy Spirit upon conversion—the believing Samaritans received the Spirit (Acts 8:16-18), upon his conversion Paul received the Holy Spirit (Acts 9:17), the astonished Jewish Christians were witnesses to God giving the Spirit to the Gentiles when Peter preached to Cornelius (Acts 10:44-45), and at the Jerusalem conference the apostles affirmed the giving of the Holy Spirit to both Jews and Gentiles (Acts 15:8).

The *key* to this fresh emphasis on the abiding, indwelling presence of the Spirit is found on two levels. First, the Holy Spirit is felt to possess the character of Jesus, therefore, any spirit contrary to that of Jesus cannot be the Holy Spirit. Secondly, the Spirit is poured out on the believers as a direct fulfillment of prophecy.

When Peter spoke of the promise (Acts 2:39), he was referring to the promise of the pouring out of God's Holy Spirit in the last days. He earlier quoted the prophet Joel (Acts 2:16-21 and Joel 2:28-32) in this connection. The materialistic promises of a golden age which Israel earlier sought had been gradually reinterpreted to include, as an important part, the outpouring of God's Spirit on all His people in the messianic age (when the Messiah would come). The proclamation of John the Baptist, of Jesus, and of the early church was that this messianic age had arrived in Jesus; that God was pouring out His Spirit on His church!

Whereas in the Old Testament the Spirit fell on the few in an involuntary way, we see in the New Testament that all Christians receive the Holy Spirit by a voluntary act of faith through trust in Jesus for salvation. The Holy Spirit is a gift of God given to us as a direct result of our hearing the gospel and responding in faith, as a result of our voluntary dying and rising with our Lord Jesus (Gal. 3:2; Rom. 6:1-11; 8:10-11).

Presence and Control

Every believer has the Holy Spirit dwelling in him as the result of a deliberate choice to repent of personal sins and to turn in faith to Jesus. And, if the Holy Spirit is to have a larger part in our lives than mere presence (I use the word *mere* not as a belittling term, but to show limitation), a presence of which we may not even be aware—we will have to make a deliberate choice and take definite steps. We must allow, even invite, the Holy Spirit to control our lives.

Perhaps the difference between *presence* and *control* of the Spirit may be seen in the analogy of our taking someone into our home. A few years ago my family had a student from Sweden as our houseguest for a school term. She had the full use of the house, as a member of our family. It would have been both sad and silly if we had confined her to the living room or to her bedroom. In the same kind of terms, the Book of Revelation says that Jesus knocks at our hearts' doors. When we respond in faith and invite the Holy Spirit to come into our lives, we have another decision to make concerning whether we will allow Him to have full control and use of our lives. He is not automatically in control of our daily lives. Only when we gladly invite Him into all areas of our lives, and allow Him to shape our lives, is He really Lord.

When we speak of the control of our lives by the Holy Spirit we are speaking of an empowering presence within us, enabling us to be the channels of God's grace. The control of the Spirit means a new set of values acted upon—"Set your minds on things above." The control of the Spirit means the discovery and use of spiritual gifts. The control of the Spirit means a deepened desire, which is fulfilled, for more knowledge of the Lord Jesus and fellowship with Him. The control of the Spirit is not a terrifying possibility, but rather a means of our spiritual development which God intends. The Spirit's control of our life is as sails to a ship or wings to a bird.

Who Controls My Life?

The foundational question of this book is: Who controls my life? The basic decision concerning the spiritual depth of the Christian—his life in the Spirit—is summed up in that question. In the stirring Philippian passage in which Paul spoke of pressing toward the mark, and of giving up all things for Jesus' sake, he spoke of "laying hold upon" or "grasping" God's intention for his life. Interestingly, he said, "I follow after, if that I might *lay hold upon* that for which *I have been laid hold upon* by Christ Jesus" (3:12, author's translation and italics). We have, indeed, been laid hold upon by the Holy Spirit. Yet, there must be a conscious choice on our part if the Spirit is to have control of our lives. Is the Holy Spirit confined to the role of an observer through mere presence in your life, or is He a dynamic, shaping, controlling force in your life? The Holy Spirit cannot fill and control an unwilling, unsubmitted, uncommitted life.

The Spirit seeks to put our whole lives—physical, emotional, mental, and spiritual—under the will of God. Only then can Paul's victorious claim be ours: "I am crucified with Christ: nevertheless I live, yet not I, but Christ liveth in me: and the life I now live in the flesh I live by the faith of the Son of God, who loved me, and gave himself for me" (Gal. 2:20). No one ever crucified himself! Crucifixion of self is the work of the Holy Spirit, and then only when we ask Him to do so, that Jesus might live in us each day in a way supremely pleasing to God.

Taking Spiritual Inventory

Before Christians can deepen their lives in the Spirit, they must realize who the Spirit is and what He wishes to accomplish in their lives. There must also be a desire to experience a deeper life in the Spirit before any changes can come about. This desire leads to the conscious decision on the part of the growing Christians to let Jesus Christ rule in their lives.

In that light, most of us need to take a spiritual inventory of our lives at regular intervals. Even the simplest inventory will make most of us blush spiritually. For instance, ask yourself the following questions and grade yourself on a scale of 1 to 4 (1-sometimes, 2-often, 3-usually, and 4-always):

> I love Jesus more than I love myself or anyone else.
> Christ is the center of my personality.
> I am obedient to God's will.
> I feel the presence of Jesus in my life.

See what I mean about even the simplest spiritual checkup giving us cause for alarm?

In a manner of speaking, the following chapters of this book are a spiritual inventory. As you read each chapter, let it lead you to a spiritual inventory of your life in the Spirit. You have already wrestled with the foundational question of the book: Who controls my life? Other chapters will confront you with these questions: What does life in the Spirit look like? What decides the shape of my spiritual life? Am I a person of prayer? Am I a fruitful Christian? Is my church guided by the Spirit? Is there any conflict with the devil? The final chapter is not a question, but rather explores the earnest expectation with which Paul crowned his soaring chapter on the Spirit, Romans 8: Tell me again about the promised victory!

Notes

1. H. Wheeler Robinson, *The Christian Experience of the Holy Spirit*, p. 11.

2. *Life and Diary of David Brainerd* (Grand Rapids: Sovereign Grace Publishers, 1971), pp. 20-21.

3. Ibid., p. 140.

4. V. Raymond Edman, *They Found the Secret* (Grand Rapids: Zondervan Publishing House, 1960), pp. 97-98 (an excellent collection of case studies of life in the Spirit).

5. A. J. Gordon, *How Christ Came to Church* (Philadelphia: American Baptist Publication society, 1896). pp. 28-32.

6. W. Garden Blaikie. *The Personal Life of David Livingstone* (New York: Fleming H. Revell Company, n.d. [ca. 1880]), p. 490.

7. Ibid., p. 197.

8. Ibid., p. 453.

9. Mary Bosanquet, *The Life and Death of Dietrich Bonhoeffer* (New York: Harper and Row, 1968), p. 74.

10. Ibid., p. 263.

11. Ibid., p. 271, 272

12. Ibid., p. 15.

13. For a further discussion of the term *Paraclete*, see Raymond E. Brown, *The Gospel According to John (XIII-XXI)*, The Anchor Bible Commentary (Garden City: Doubleday and Company, Inc., 1970), pp. 1136-43.

14. Quoted in John Randolph Taylor, *God Loves Like That!* (Richmond: John Knox Press, 1962), p. 106.

15. Frank Stagg, *The Holy Spirit Today*, pp. 18-19.

2

The Description
What Does Life
in the Spirit Look Like?

How does one describe a way of life both so common and so unusual as the life in the Holy Spirit? It is so common in that many of you who read this page have been surrounded with evidences of the life in the Spirit as long as you can remember, for you were brought up in a Christian family and nourished in the church. Because familiarity often leads to blindness, much of what would be astounding to the unconverted, if he could experience it, is often overlooked by Christians. Then, too, many Christians are not sure their lives reflect the qualities of lives redeemed and controlled by the Spirit.

This chapter looks at some of the biblical images used to describe life in the Spirit. The New Testament uses many names for the Holy Spirit and His work in the life of both the individual believer and the church as a whole.

The "Holy" Spirit

Some of the designations used for the Holy Spirit in the New Testament include: Holy Ghost (KJV), Spirit which is of God, Holy Spirit of promise, eternal Spirit, Spirit of grace, Spirit of Christ, Spirit of holiness, Spirit of Life, Spirit, Spirit of our God, and Spirit of the Lord. In this book, for clarity, the terms *Holy Spirit* and *Spirit* will be used interchangeably to speak of the presence and work of the third Person of the Trinity.

The variety of names for the Spirit comes from the richness of the experience of the early Christians. The Spirit was a vital reality. Paul referred to the Spirit's work over one hundred times in his letters—some nineteen times in the eighth chapter of Romans alone. Twenty-three of the twenty-seven books of the New Testament mention the work of the

Spirit. If you were writing letters such as Paul wrote, what name would you give to the Holy Spirit based upon your experience of Him?

Life in the Spirit begins with the basic idea of life set apart from the world, yet bound together with all other Christians to make up the church. Three other perspectives help describe life in the Spirit: looking back, looking ahead, and looking inward.

The Separated Life of Holiness

The Ground of Holiness

Obviously the Holy Spirit cannot inhabit unholy people. The reason is bound up in the meaning of "Holy" Spirit. What do we mean by "Holy" Spirit? A family of words dealing with the idea of "Holy" may be translated as *holiness, sanctification, consecration,* and *saint.*

Long ago the idea of *holy* was simply "awe"; something holy was something to be given plenty of room. Maybe the thing or person was cursed or reverenced. In religious connections, the idea of holiness had to do with being separated from ordinary life. Holiness did not necessarily mean moral, since pagan temple prostitutes were considered to be holy, set apart.

In the Old Testament, holiness, while definitely carrying the idea of being separated and set apart from daily life, also has a moral flavor. When God made the covenant with Israel, He set the band of runaway slaves apart and and also laid on them the responsibility of morality: "For I am the Lord, that bringeth you up out of the land of Egypt, to be your God: *ye shall therefore be holy, for I am holy*" (Lev. 11:45, author's italics).

Biblical holiness, then, has a moral quality which is derived from the very character of God. A kindred idea which may help in understanding holiness is the Latin background of the English word *sacred,* which is from a root meaning to be whole or sound. So we see that holiness has to do with being set apart, having a moral character and requirement based on God's nature, and possessing wholeness and soundness.

The Holy Spirit, as one person of the Trinity through whom we experience God, reflects that holy nature of God as being set apart from the sinful world humanity has made of God's perfect creation. The Spirit comes into this world to reveal the holiness of God, to convict the world of sin, to witness to our hearts of the plan and provision of God for salvation, and to indwell those who respond in faith so that they may be holy and be conformed to the image of Jesus.

Since the Holy Spirit is God, He could not live in the life of an unholy person. The Christian, then, is changed from an unholy person to a holy person by the Spirit in the work of conversion. "For this is the will of God, even your sanctification" (1 Thess. 4:3).

The Baptism of the Spirit

The change from an unholy person to a holy person is a part of what the New Testament calls the baptism of the Holy Spirit. Many people are confused about this baptism, because we have read our own meanings into the biblical account. For instance, we are never told in Scripture to seek this baptism; nor is it a special blessing or gift for only a chosen few, but rather is a part of every Christian's experience of conversion.

We must let the New Testament define baptism of the Holy Spirit. In reporting the preaching of John, all four Gospels mention the promise that Jesus would baptize with the Holy Spirit. While the Gospels say remarkably little about the fulfillment of this baptism with the Spirit, John 3 tells us more about how the Baptist's words are to be understood. To Nicodemus's question about the impossibility of being born again, Jesus replied,

> Verily, verily, I say unto thee, Except a man be born again, he cannot see the kingdom of God. Nicodemus saith unto him, How can a man be born when he is old? . . . Jesus answered, Verily, verily, I say unto thee, Except a man be born of water and of the Spirit, he cannot enter into the kingdom of God. Marvel not that I said unto thee, Ye must be born again. The wind bloweth where it listeth, and thou hearest the sound thereof, but canst not tell whence it cometh, and whither it goeth: so is every one that is born of the Spirit (vv. 3-5,7-8).

When persons are baptized with the Holy Spirit, they are born anew of the Spirit.

This promise of the baptism of the Spirit is stated again in Acts 1:5 in the light of its coming fulfillment for those who were Christ's at Pentecost: "For John truly baptized with water; but ye shall be baptized with the Holy [Spirit] not many days hence."

Another fulfillment of this promise of the baptism of the Spirit was seen by Peter in the conversion of Cornelius and those with him. Here is how Peter told the Jerusalem church about that remarkable experience:

> And as I began to speak, the Holy Ghost fell on them, as on us at the beginning. Then remembered I the word of the Lord, how that he said, John indeed baptized with water; but ye shall be baptized with the Holy Ghost. Forasmuch then as God gave them the like gift as he did unto us, who believed on the Lord Jesus Christ; what was I, that I could withstand God? When they heard these things, they held their peace, and glorified God, saying, Then hath God also to the Gentiles granted repentance unto life (Acts 11:15-18).

Other references which deal with the baptism of the Spirit include Romans 6:3-4; 1 Corinthians 12:13; Galatians 3:27; Ephesians 4:5; and Colossians 2:12. From these Scriptures, which speak of both the water baptism and the Spirit baptism of which the water is a symbol, we see that the baptism of the Spirit brings the death and resurrection of Jesus into effect in the life of the believer. It is also clear that the baptism of the Spirit focuses on the formation of the body of Christ of those who commit themselves to Him.

The baptism of the Holy Spirit is a result of the conversion experience. When we repent of our sins (our deeds) and our sin (our rebellious stance against God) and turn in faith to Jesus, we are both reconciled with God and baptized into the Holy Spirit. Reconcilliation cuts through the grain of our previous existence; it upsets our old life and claims us and issues in the the reality of the reshaping work of the baptism of the Spirit. "God hath from the beginning chosen you to salvation through sanctification of the Spirit and belief of the truth" (2 Thess. 2:13). We may think of this baptism as the inner transformation of our lives with three aspects: the imparting of a new nature, the separation from the world, and the new standing of holiness.

The new nature.—The baptism of the Spirit gives us a new nature: "Therefore if any man be in Christ, he is a new creature: old things are passed away; behold, all things are become new" (2 Cor. 5:17). Our new nature is one of love, trust, and peace toward God, and agape love for other people. The rebellious, self-centered nature is exchanged through our baptism into Christ by the Holy Spirit. Our new nature must be developed as we live. This is the reality of sanctification and brings us face to face with the problem of Christian obedience. We develop our new nature as we respond to the Spirit within, as we separate ourselves from the world, and as we accept in the midst of our humanity and frailty the new standing of holiness in which God has placed us.

The separation from the world.—This reality is a result of the change of our nature through the Holy Spirit. We no longer desire the sinful way of the unconverted. More than a mere washing up of our lives has taken place. Conversion is more than just turning over a new moral leaf. Our "wanters" are changed, and we no longer want to be and do what we once did.

Separation from the world is always more a challenge than an accomplished fact. We are challenged by God's summons to be shaped by the Spirit in the likeness of "his Son, that he might be the firstborn among many brethren" (Rom. 8:29). Still we struggle, knowing that, in the words of Calvin's sermon, "We have to reflect that God would not be placated even with the holiness of angels, if He should call for the most exact sifting of their works."[1] And again, "We hold that there is not a single action performed by saints which, if judged in itself, does not merit a just reward of shame."[2]

The glory of our separation from the world lies in our understanding that the work of sanctification, of separation, is a work of God. As Luther said, "Christian holiness is not active but passive."[3] We are the vessels of God in this world, being filled and used at the direction of the Holy Spirit, in accordance with our willingness.

The new standing of holiness.—In the baptism of the Spirit, we receive a new standing of holiness. While the separation of our lives and desires from the fleshly desires of the world may be seen as one side of our baptism in the Spirit, the negative side, there is a positive side revealed in our new standing before God as a holy person. God "hath saved us, and called us with a holy calling, not according to our works, but according to his own purpose and grace, which was given us in Christ Jesus before the world began" (2 Tim. 1:9). Peter told us that we are "a chosen generation, a royal priesthood, an *holy* nation, a peculiar people; that ye should shew forth the praises of him who called you out of darkness into his marvelous light" (1 Pet. 2:9, author's italics).

Somewhere I read about a man of meager education and means who was ministered to and led to the Lord by a neighborhood church. He overflowed with the joy of his salvation and the fellowship of his new friends. One night he confided to his wife that he wanted so badly to be a part of the church softball team but had no jersey with writing on it like the other men. His dear wife could read no better than he, but she determined to sew him a jersey and put some writing on it, so he would be as properly outfitted as the other men. As she sewed one day, she saw a bright new sign being put in the window of a grocery across the street. The writing on the sign looked good to her, although she hadn't the faintest idea what it said. So she sewed the same letters onto her her husband's jersey and proudly presented it to him. He wore it just as proudly to play the next game with his church ball team. Nobody laughed, for they all knew that he was indeed "Under New Management" since giving his heart to Jesus! And that's what the baptism of the Spirit means!

The Baptism of the Spirit and the Filling of the Spirit

Often people are confused about the filling of the Spirit and the baptism of the Spirit. Are they the one and the same? Can we be filled over and over? Does the Spirit leave a Christian? Is there a need to be baptized in the Holy Spirit and over? Is one of these terms another way to express a second stage in our spiritual pilgrimage?

Several major differences exist between the baptism and the filling of the Spirit. The baptism of the Spirit is something the Holy Spirit does to us; it is the placing of each of us into a special relationship to our Lord and His church at the time of conversation. This is clearly a once-for-all, unique event. We are baptized by the Spirit when we are saved. On the other hand, we are commanded to be filled with the Spirit (Eph. 5:18). The filling of the Spirit is something we can have some control over, and we are not pleasing to God if we are not filled with the Spirit.

To be filled with the Spirit does not mean we get more of the Spirit; it rather means the Spirit gets more of us! The filling is a sense of empowering and equipping, often for a special task, such as the Pentecost experience of preaching in other languages (Acts 2) or Peter being filled with the Spirit as he answered charges before the high priest (Acts 4:8). Filling is dependent upon our surrender to the Holy Spirit.

Every Christian has the Holy Spirit residing in his or her life, but not every Christian allows the Spirit to control his or her life by providing wisdom and strength in times of special tasks or crises. Over and over we can come to God in prayer and again turn over our lives to Him and find fresh filling, or controlling, of the Spirit. We must be filled over and over.

Point and Process

So our state of holiness, our set apartness, is first a status or position in which we are put as part of the meaning of conversion, as a result of our baptism in the Holy Spirit. "But ye are washed, but ye are sanctified, but ye are justified in the name of the Lord Jesus, and by the Spirit of our God" (1 Cor. 6:11). This state of holiness given at conversion is called sanctification and is God's doing.

Sanctification is a state or position or status—a point from which something else is intended to take place. We do not grow into sanctification; but once God has placed us in that state through conversion, we are expected to grow in sanctification. For instance, a bystander cannot suddenly walk up to the starting line of an Olympic race and run with the contenders; something must take place first. But when those requirements are met and he finds himself on the mark, toes on the starting block, lane line stretching out ahead, and the starter gun sounds—he must put all his strength into the race. While he could never have run without being admitted to the lineup, likewise he will never win just standing at the starting mark. He must run!

There is a growth in holiness which is a part of our working out the moral demands of God who has set us apart. "But as he which hath called you is holy, so be ye holy in all manner of conversation; Because it is written, Be ye holy; for I am holy" (1. Pet. 1:15-16).

Now, this state of holiness, this set apartness from the world and a new nature and awareness of God's ethical demands, does not mean that we are automatically made sinless. The imperfection of our obedience as Christians is known to each of us. The church in Corinth was composed of very imperfect people—they had divided into church factions, there was apparently gross immorality among some members, the fellowship was injured by lawsuits, there were questions about the sexual relationship in marriage, distortion of the Lord's Supper, misuse of spiritual gifts, and misunderstanding of the doctrine of the resurrection of the dead. Yet Paul began his letter dealing with these matters in this manner: "Unto the church of God which is at Corinth, to them that are *sanctified* in Christ Jesus, called to be *saints*" (1 Cor. 1:2, author's italics). While

Paul did not ignore or condone their sins, he still called these Corinthians saints. They were not perfect, only set apart from the world. They had been sanctified, and Paul called them to truly live like saints. We see the same imperfection and inability and unwillingness to completely separate ourselves from the world in the piercing comment Paul made to the Galatians who were being influenced by legalism: "Are ye so foolish? having begun in the Spirit, are ye now made perfect by the flesh?" (Gal. 3:3).

Sanctification is both gift and demand, point and call to progress. Peter expressed this call to progress in holiness when he wrote to the scattered Christians of Asia Minor, calling them "elect [called, chosen] according to the foreknowledge of God the Father, through sanctification [setting apart] of the Spirit, unto obedience (1 Pet. 1:2). We are sanctified from the moment of our baptism of the Spirit and are moving from that point to a state of perfection which we will fully reach only when we stand before God on the last day.

There is also a *hidden* aspect to our separation from the world. We are not called to leave this world, nor to look or dress oddly, but to be a separate people inside. We are to remain in the midst of the world, as the salt and light. We are mixed in with the world, yet separated by our very natures.

Bound in the Same Bundle

Our sanctification, our holiness, involves a separation from the world. Not a total separation, but one involving our minds, wills, and bodies. This aspect of sanctification is but half the baptism of the Spirit. The other half is that of togetherness. We are called *from* the world and *to* the fellowship of other saints by the Spirit. The intention of the Holy Spirit is to bind all believers together in one bundle as the church, the body of Christ: past, present, and future.

Apostolic letters began by reminding the readers that they were called to be saints together, as part of the church. The New Testament was not written in terms of the solitary Christian; all its Christians were either members of a church or heading that way as fast as they could! The unity of the church, both local and universal, is described in terms of all Christians being one "loaf"; and in the context of spiritual gifts, Paul said, "by one Spirit are we all baptized into one body" (1 Cor. 12:13).

Paul spoke of the unique fellowship of our common bond in Christ as he appealed from prison to the church at Philippi: "If there be . . . any fellowship of the Spirit, . . . Fulfil ye my joy, that ye be likeminded" (Phil. 2:1-2). The word "if" in the King James Version is an accurate rendering of the Greek, but carries an element of uncertainty not intended by the Greek. Perhaps a clearer phrasing would be "*since* there is a fellowship of the Spirit. . . ." The appeal to unity is based upon their experience of fellowship together in the Lord.

A depth of fellowship and unity exists among Christian brothers and sisters that is deeper and more meaningful than the world can offer. By the grace of the Holy Spirit, I am made deeply aware of our fellowship in Christ when we celebrate the Lord's Supper. As I look out over the congregation and reflect on the sorrows, on the deep courage and faith, on the burdens shared only with God and pastor, I am conscious of a tie, not of this world, that binds us together. As our deacons march down the long center aisle of our church to the Lord's Supper table after serving the congregation, I feel a great love for them, my colleagues in ministry, who are in this world but not of this world. Together, we have been called out of darkness into the circle of light, into the kingdom of His dear Son.

My family and I have also worshiped with another denomination and received Communion with these fellow believers at the midnight hour. And the realization of the vast fellowship of the Holy Spirit, deep and eternal, flooded over me. When this old world has been folded up and flung away like a worn-out, old coat, our fellowship in Christ by the Holy Spirit will remain pure and eternal.

We are all bound in one bundle in Christ! Concerning all these aspects of our sanctification, then, let us remember the beautiful prayer of Paul on behalf of the Christians in the Thessalonian church: "And the very God of peace sanctify you wholly; and I pray God your whole spirit and soul and body be preserved blameless unto the coming of our Lord Jesus Christ. Faithful is he that calleth you, who also will do it" (1 Thess. 5:23-24).

Looking Back: Contrasts

One of the best and most obvious ways to describe the new life in the Spirit is by contrast with the old life. A sort of religious before-and-after portrait. The major contrast of the New Testament is Paul's description of life in the Spirit as opposed to life in the flesh. Other contrasts of the pre-Christian life with the life in Christ include the old man and the new man and the dead man and the alive man and the unwashed and the "washed" life.

Flesh and Spirit

The flesh.—While this contrast is woven throughout Paul's writings, the most prominent passages illustrating the contrast of flesh and Spirit are Romans 7:14-25; 8:1-13; and Galatians 5:13-26. We should keep in mind that flesh in the New Testament may have one of several different meanings. The word can be used in the literal and natural sense as the substance of our body. Sometimes *flesh* is used when speaking of seeing things from a purely human point of view, as opposed to the view of God. Often the word *flesh* has ethical meaning as when we speak of sins of the flesh or life in the flesh. Too often we restrict sins of the flesh to misdeeds of a sexual nature, when the New Testament insists that those sins we would deem "spiritual" sins (that is, jealousy, anger, and so forth) are rooted in the flesh.

No one statement can possibly sum up the essence of flesh in this ethical sense. The flesh is our lower nature with its instincts and desires, but to simply say this does not go far enough. To live according to the flesh is to live without faith in God. We can be ever so moral and upright and kind, but if life has no vertical dimension, no relationship of faith toward Christ, we are living in the flesh. We may say that flesh stands for human nature in its frailty and weakness; and that flesh is the part of our nature which willingly surrenders to sin and works with evil. The flesh is the bridgehead for the devil, the traitor within, who opens the gates for the enemy.

Flesh represents the complete inadequacy of persons when they stand before God. Life in the flesh cannot please God, nor is there a desire in this realm of existence to do so. Flesh is a symbol for our slavery to sin, our powerlessness to do the good we may even wish to do.

The Spirit.—In contrast, life in the Spirit is a life surrendered to Jesus in repentance and faith. It is a life indwelt by the Spirit. It may be helpful to compare the cases of those in the Gospels who were indwelt, possessed, by evil spirits. You remember that Jesus, in delivering these persons, spoke directly to the evil spirits, for the evil spirits were in control, not the persons (Mark 1:25; 5:8,12-13). Being in the Spirit is the same situation in a very positive sense, for the existence of the believer is determined by the Holy Spirit within. The Spirit is the supernatural element breaking into our lives to free us from the control of the perishing flesh. Domination of the Spirit replaces the domination of the flesh.

In fact, the Spirit is the energizing force which enables the Christian to give up the old desires, to lay down the arms of rebellion against God. To live in the Spirit is to cease boasting in the flesh (compare Phil. 3:4-7), to cease fulfilling the desires of the flesh, and to refocus life on the things of the Spirit. Living in the Spirit allows believers to see life in the flesh as the Satan-manipulated existence that it really is and to turn from this puppet-like life to the authentic existence of life in the Spirit.

Life led by the Spirit is life filled with peace and joy and life characterized by the fruit of the Spirit (Gal. 5:22-23; Rom. 6:22; 14:17). It is life lived in spiritual freedom from the law of sin and death (Rom. 8:2; 2 Cor. 3:17); we are no longer slaves to sin nor do we live in fear of death. Contrary to the life of the flesh, life in the Spirit is pleasing to God (Rom. 8:5-9).

As Christians who live in the Spirit, we have resources available—the power and presence of the Spirit within us (Phil. 1:19)—to defeat the flesh. A conflict between flesh and Spirit continues while we are in this world. Thus we are urged: "If we live in the Spirit, let us also walk in the Spirit" (Gal. 5:25). We are admonished, "Walk in the Spirit, and ye shall not fulfil the lust of the flesh" (v. 16). The imperatives of the Christian life are very much needed, "If ye then be risen with Christ, seek those things which are above" (Col. 3:1).

The images *walk* and *be led* speak of the habitual patterns of our lives. A person walks, or lives, in the path fashioned by habits and desires. We are admonished over and over to establish patterns of daily life in accordance with the Spirit, not the flesh. We are led either by the Spirit or by the flesh.

Old Man/New Man and Dead Man/Alive Man

Much similarity exists between the two contrasting images of old man and new man and dead man and alive man. Often the same Scriptures picture both images, for the reality behind both is the same—the great contrast through the Spirit.

Old man and new man.—The old man is another way of speaking of the pre-Christian life-style and mind-set. The contrast is between the evil (old man), and the good (new man) between the flesh and the Spirit. The old and the new are mutually exclusive. The old man is characterized by the corruption of the lusts of deceit, by sins both of body and spirit (Col 3:8-9; Eph. 4:22).

In the three passages dealing with the contrast of old man and new man, newness stands for the reality of salvation which the Christian has in Christ. The mark of the new man is that he is being created in the image of God—that image which had been blurred by sin. The new man is being changed into the image of the Lord (Christ) from glory to glory (2 Cor. 3:18). The model, and complete and perfect new man, is Christ (Rom. 8:28-31).

This image of the old man and the new man is found in three passages in the New Testament—Romans 6:6; Colossians 3:9-10; and Ephesians 4:22-24. Romans 6:6 tells us that our old man (self) has been crucified with Christ. The two other passages make an appeal for holy living based on the crucifixion of the old man we once were.

Dead man and alive man.—The concept of being crucified with Christ brings us to the image of dead and alive men. The term "dead" man as experienced in the Christian life has reference to several things. First, it is a dying to or from something, such as a dying to sin (Rom. 6:2), self (2 Cor. 5:14-15), the law (Rom. 7:6; Gal. 2:19), the deeds of the flesh (Rom. 8:13), or the world (Col. 2:20; 3:3). It is also a dying with Christ, as Romans 6 pictures. Dying with Christ removes us from the power of the flesh, the world, the devil, and any other powers or rulers of this world (Col. 2:20).

We must realize that the Holy Spirit is the source of power which enables us both to die to sin through crucifixion with Christ and to be raised with Him (Rom. 8:13). We must realize that there is no dying to sin apart from Christ and no resurrection apart from Christ (Eph. 2:1-7; Rom. 8:13; 6:1-13; Col. 3:1-10). In Romans 6 we see water baptism used as a symbol of our baptism by the Spirit into Jesus' death. We are united with Him in His death in a real and mystical sense.

As Jesus' death means the death of our old selves, so His resurrection means bringing to life the new persons in this present existence as well as the redemption of the body on the last day. In Christ we have passed from death into life both in the ethical sphere and in regard to physical death.

To be alive means to "walk in newness of life" (Rom. 6:4), to live life in accordance with the guidance of the Spirit. To be alive means to put to death the deeds of the body (Rom. 8:13). To be alive means to set our thoughts and desires on spiritual things, on things above (Col. 3:1). To be alive means to present ourselves to God as those considered dead but suddenly knocking at the front door—because of Christ's death on our behalf (Rom. 6:13)—and reporting for duty. To be alive means that we look upon ourselves as dead to this world's lusts (v. 11). This statement is important, for we do not have the strength in ourselves to put our sinful nature to death. Nobody ever crucified himself—this is the work of the Holy Spirit. And it is possible only where there is the desire to see this death take place; where the person "considers" himself dead to sin through Christ.

The Washed Life

A most common yet powerful contrast between the nonbeliever and the Christian is seen in the unclean life and the washed, or sanctified life. The New Testament abounds with references to the unsaved life of uncleanness (Rom. 1:24 f.; 6:19; 2 Cor. 12:21; 1 Thess. 2:3; Eph. 4:19; 5:3,5). These verses give a general description of absolute separation from God, expressing the nature of a person whose actions are determined by lusts. This uncleanness is a clinging, infecting force, and is the direct opposite of the sanctified life bestowed by the Holy Spirit.

We are helped in our understanding of the life in the Spirit through various Scriptures related to the cleansed life (Eph. 5:26; 1 Cor. 6:11; Titus 3:5; 1 Pet. 1:2; 1 John 1:7; and Rev. 1:5 [washed or loosed]). The washings in these Scriptures seem to have three backgrounds. The first is a general use of the metaphor of washing to cleanse from the filth and unbelief of the old life. The second background is the act of baptism, a symbolic and mystical washing (1 Cor. 6:11; Titus 3:5; Eph. 5:26). The third background is the Jewish sacrificial ceremony of sprinkling half the blood of the sacrifice on the altar and half on the people, through which they are ritually cleansed (1 Pet. 1:2; 1 John 1:7; Rev. 1:5).

This cleansing of our lives, as part of our conversion, is the work of the Holy Spirit; all human effort is of no avail in really cleansing us. Two distinct actions take place at the same time: cleansing from the old life, and consecration to the new existence.

The study of the image of washing should spur us to a more holy life through the Spirit. "But ye are washed, but ye are sanctified, but ye are justified in the name of the Lord Jesus, and by the Spirit of our God" (1 Cor. 6:11). "[Glory and dominion for ever and ever] Unto him that loved us, and washed us from our sins in his own blood" (Rev. 1:5).

Looking Within: Power

To read Paul's prayers forces us to ask ourselves if we have experienced that inner power of which he wrote: "That he would grant you, according to the riches of his glory, to be strengthened with might by his Spirit in the inner man" (Eph. 3:16); "[that you may know] what is the exceeding greatness of his power to us-ward who believe, according to the working of his mighty power, Which he wrought in Christ, when he raised him from the dead" (Eph. 1:19-20); "I can do all things through Christ which strengtheneth me" (Phil. 4:13); and "[that you be] Strengthened with all might, according to his glorious power" (Col. 1:11).

The Enabling Spirit

We are told in 2 Timothy, "God hath not given us the Spirit of fear; but of power, and of love, and of a sound mind" (1:7). In the New Testament, we see that God is concerned that our knowledge and understanding of this power be complete, so the Spirit can perfect the work He intends in us. This great power of which Paul spoke is the same power which raised Jesus from the dead, and the same power which raises us from the old life and shapes our new life. Thus the Holy Spirit is the enabler. The poem of John Drinkwater expresses clearly our need in this area:

> Grant us the will to fashion as we feel,
> Grant us the strength to labour as we know,
> Grant us the purpose, ribbed and edged with steel,
>   To strike the blow.
> Knowledge we ask not—knowledge Thou has lent;
> But Lord, the will—there lies our bitter need.
> Give us to build above the deep intent
>   The deed, the deed.[4]

And this is exactly the empowering work of the Spirit. He gives power both for doing and becoming.

It seems to me that the two directions of the Spirit's empowering work are well expressed as outward power in Acts 1:8: "But ye shall receive power, after that the Holy [Spirit] is come upon you: and ye shall be my witnesses" and as inward power in John 1:12: "But as many as received him, to them gave he power to become the sons of God." Where the Spirit is, there is power, in both an inward and outward directed sense. The outward use of power is in preaching, mighty deeds, and healing, while the inward power is demonstrated in the reshaping and strengthening of our lives (1 Cor. 2:4; Rom. 15:19).

The Sphere of the Spirit's Power

From the Scriptures we learn that this great power of the resurrection bestowed through the Spirit limits itself to operation in the weakness of our life. That is, the power of the Spirit works in those who are seen as weak by the world. This power is a concealed, invisible power. The hidden aspect is supremely seen in the apparent weakness of the death of Jesus on the cross, while the authentic power is openly displayed in the resurrection. The reason is clear: "He said unto me, my grace is sufficient for thee: for *my strength is made perfect in weakness*. Most gladly, therefore will I rather glory in my infirmities, that the power of Christ may rest upon me . . . for when I am weak, then am I strong" (2 Cor. 12:9-10, author's italics).

This working of power through earthly weakness is a deliberate choice God has made which calls for the full cooperation of the believer: "For ye see your calling, brethren, how that not many wise men after the flesh, not many mighty, not many noble, are called: But . . . God hath chosen the weak things of the world to confound the things which are mighty" (1 Cor. 1:26-27).

The Power to Become the Temple of God

The image of our being the temple, the dwelling place of God both individually, and collectively as the church, is a beautiful and demanding concept. Jewish thought in the time of Jesus included the idea that God would build in the last days a magnificent, new, perfect temple in which

He would dwell. The early Christians realized the last days were taking place, and they also realized that the idea of a physical temple as a habitation for God would not be fulfilled, as Stephen declared: "Howbeit the most High dwelleth not in temples made with hands" (Acts 7:48). They knew the temple was a spiritual one, and in passages such as 1 Corinthians 3:16; 6:19; 2 Corinthians 6:16-17; Ephesians 2:19-22; and 1 Peter 2:5-6, we learn of our role as believers in becoming the spiritual dwelling place of God.

The Holy Spirit is our power to become this house of God: "In whom [Jesus] ye also are builded together for an habitation of God through the Spirit" (Eph. 2:22). For God to truly dwell in our bodies and lives, several things become evident. First, we must be holy. We must be not only in the state of holiness, that is, sanctification, but also we must be continually separating and renewing our life through the Spirit. Paul kept reminding the Corinthian Christians: "What? know ye not that your body is the temple of the Holy Spirit which is in you?" (1 Cor. 6:19; see also 1 Cor. 3:16). We must not abuse, misuse, or defile our bodies. We must purify our minds, if our life is God's home. Our hearts must likewise be kept free of unclean desires. This is more than a request of us; it is a demand: "If any man defile the temple of God, him shall God destroy; for the temple of God is holy, which temple ye are" (1 Cor. 3:17). Second, if God has taken residence in our life and body, we no longer belong to ourselves, but to God (1 Cor. 6:19). We are bought with a price, and must glorify God in soul and body.

George MacDonald has a story which underlines the truth that this building of a temple is not possible through our own efforts, nor is that intended. Through the power of the Holy Spirit, we become God's dwelling place. As MacDonald describes it, imagine that you are a house. God comes to rebuild the house, and at first what he does is clear to you. He fixes the roof, repairs the drains, and all that. Those things needed doing, and you are even pleased. But it is not long before He begins repairs that are more in depth, that do not make sense to us, and even hurt! What is the meaning of all this? He explains to you that His plan for rebuilding and enlarging is not the same as your expectations—adding on a little here and there. His intention is not just a little cottage, but a palace in which *He* will come to live! How true that analogy is! His plan is not our plan, and we have not the power to build the temple.

The Power to Pray

We need to see the relationship of the Spirit to the believer's prayer life. C. H. Dodd spoke of Holy-Spirit-led prayer as "the divine in us appealing to the God above us."[5] As in other areas of the Christian's life, so also in prayer the Holy Spirit takes the initiative.

The Spirit's power is revealed in our weaknesses, and this is so true in prayer. "Likewise the Spirit also helpeth our infirmities: for we know not what we should pray for as we ought: but the Spirit itself maketh intercession for us with groanings which cannot be uttered" (Rom. 8:26). Prayer takes on a supernatural aspect when the Spirit intercedes for us. Have we never been so burdened, so confused, so weary that our prayers could only be "Oh, My Father!" In such times, that deep cry of the heart is interpreted and voiced, unheard by us, through the Holy Spirit to the eternal Father.

In Ephesians we have the admonition not to be drunk with wine, but rather be filled with the Spirit, which in that particular passage is interpreted to mean speaking in psalms and hymns, singing, and giving thanks always to God (5:18-20). The Spirit encourages our prayers. Jude 20 speaks also of our praying in the Spirit as a constant act.

Access to God is another facet of the powerful working within us of the Spirit. First an access, an ushering into the presence of God as friends of the Son, is seen in a redemptive sense (1 Pet. 3:18; Rom. 5:2). Then, throughout our pilgrimage we are given access to God through prayer by the Holy Spirit. In several Scriptures, the Spirit and Christ are identified as providing access to God for the believer. "For through him [Jesus] we both have access by one Spirit unto the Father" (Eph. 2:18).

Notes

1. John Calvin, *Institutes of the Christian Religion* (Philadelphia: The Westminster Press, 1960), 1:755-756.

2. Ibid.

3. Quoted in Karl Barth, *The Holy Ghost and the Christian Life,* R. Birch Hoyle, trans. (London: Frederick Muller Limited, 1938), p. 68.

4. John Drinkwater, "A Prayer," *Masterpieces of Religious Verse,* James D. Morrison, ed., (New York: Harper and Brothers, 1948), pp. 417-18.

5. C. H. Dodd, *The Epistle of Paul to the Romans,* pp. 150-151.

3

The Dynamic
What Decides the Shape
of My Spiritual Life?

The Holy Spirit who leads us to a sense of conviction of sin, who baptizes us as responsive, repentant sinners into the body of Christ, who then takes up residence in our lives, is the same Holy Spirit who plans our spiritual maturity. He wishes to teach us all things spiritual and desires both to impart spiritual gifts and to develop and utilize those gifts. The Holy Spirit's intent is to lead us from being babes in Christ to being mature Christians.

This being true, why is it that America's largest evangelical denomination reports that 49 percent of its members are either nonresident or inactive? And probably that statistic is typical of other religious groups as well. On the other hand, why is it that some Christians stick in one's mind as spiritually mature beyond their fellow church members? I think of Russell McCoy and Arvin Stith from my seminary church, and along the way in the years since, folks like Emma Cumbie and Frances Causby. Brother McCoy was the quiet man of solid faith to whom, after everyone else had their say, the church always turned in the confidence that his words reflected a spiritual maturity. Brother Stith, over ninety years old at the time, showed his spiritual maturity by vigorously supporting the decision of the church to build a new sanctuary after he had personally strongly opposed the idea. Emma Cumbie was known as the "Chaplain of Broad Street," on which she lived, because she visited every new family and kept up with the sick, even though she was an elderly widow. Her motto: "The light that shines furtherest shines brightest at home." And Frances Causby, though confined to a wheelchair, had a very meaningful ministry through her pen. These spiritual men and women had great influence on those around them. What makes the difference?

Four Shaping Factors

The New Testament does not present a false picture of saints sailing along serenely like so many swans on a lake. It clearly describes a radical change of direction, allegiance, values, and goals of life. "For the flesh lusteth against the Spirit, and the Spirit against the flesh: and these are contrary the one to the other: so that ye cannot do the things that ye would" (Gal. 5:17). This struggle is kin to the life of a runaway salve in this country's slavery times. The slave was free, but there was a continuing danger and need for constant vigilance until he reached that land where all men were free. To update that image, we think of the words engraved on the tomb of Martin Luther King Jr.: "Free at last! Free at last! Thank God I'm free at last!" We must realize that until the Christian leaves this world he is in a struggle with the one who wishes to pull him back into bondage—the devil.

The New Testament presents a paradox about our spiritual life. It is a movement between "no longer" and "not yet." We are no longer the persons we once were, but we are not yet the persons God intends to make of us. On the one hand we hear over and over of our crucifixion with Christ, our dying with Him, our putting to death the old man we once were (see Rom. 6:2-4,6,8,11; Gal. 2:20; 5:24; 6:14; Col. 2:20; 3:3; 1 Pet. 2:24). On the other hand, we have the ringing admonitions to walk in the Spirit, to keep on putting to death the old man, to focus our thoughts above if we are truly raised with Christ, to be renewed in heart and mind (see the same Scriptures). So we are free, yet we must keep on fighting the good fight.

Our Understanding of Conversion

As I study the Bible I see at least four factors which have crucial importance in the shaping of a healthy spiritual life in the context of this struggle. The first of these is *our understanding of conversion*. The New Testament uses such phrases as *dying with Christ* and *being crucified with Him*. As Bonhoeffer said so clearly, "When Jesus calls a man, He bids him come and die." The dying with Christ must be both fact and appropriation—we must not only accept its historical nature and agree with God that Christ died for all our sins but we must also lay hold on its reality in our daily lives. The extent to which we see our daily lives truly hidden in Him shapes our spiritual existence. Like Paul we must feel that we have not only laid hold on eternal life in our confession of faith but also that we have been laid hold upon (Phil. 3:12).

A Desire to Grow Spiritually

A second shaper of the spiritual life is our *desire to grow spiritually*. At least since the second generation of Christians, the warning of the danger of complacency has been necessary: "Give the more earnest heed to the things which we have heard, lest at any time we let them slip" (Heb. 2:1), and again, "Let us hold fast the profession of our faith; . . . Not forsaking the assembling of ourselves together as the manner of some is" (Heb. 10:23,25). Peter admonished his readers: "As newborn babes, desire the sincere milk of the word, that ye may grow thereby" (1 Pet. 2:2), and Paul chided the Corinthian church: "I, brethren, could not speak unto you as unto spiritual, but as unto carnal, even as unto babes in Christ" (1 Cor. 3:1). In the letter to the Laodicean church, the risen Christ accused those Christians of being lukewarm and warned the church at Ephesus to return to its first love (Rev. 2:5; 3:15-16). Our spiritual growth is shaped by our desire to mature in Christ.

Every now and then a terrible thought comes to me: Suppose next Sunday we could see each other as God sees us spiritually. The New Testament speaks of spiritual babes—imagine deacons in diapers taking the offering from a diapered congregation! Or, heaven forbid, suppose the person in the pulpit were a baby in diapers! Unfortunately, spiritual immaturity is all too common. If we do not wish, plan, or intend to walk in the Spirit, we never will.

The Reality of the Spirit in Our Lives

The third shaping factor is the *reality of the Spirit in our lives*. For new Christians not to be taught the role of the Spirit in Christian nurture is tragic. Just as sad is for Christians to have head awareness without heart reality of the Spirit's presence! So often we feel guilty because we know our lives are not pleasing to God; we have not allowed ourselves to be crucified. So we double our efforts in our own strength, like the kitten trying harder and harder to catch its own tail or the proverbial man who tries to pull himself up by his own bootstraps. The trouble is that the power of our lives is self-generated rather than Spirit-bestowed. We fail to claim the Spirit as a reality in our daily lives. I believe this is a major cause of spiritual immaturity.

Awareness of the Holy Spirit's Role

A fourth element shaping our spiritual lives is *our awareness, or lack of awareness, of the role of the Holy Spirit*. The Holy Spirit's role is to shape the pliant believer. We have deprived ourselves of a great reservoir of power and encouragement by not emphasizing in our churches the nurturing work of the Spirit. We speak of being crucified with Christ, yet it is impossible to crucify one's own self, physically or spiritually. We speak of putting the old man to death, yet we ourselves *are* the old man that must die. We cannot do these things by ourselves. The Spirit must do these things for us. When we become aware of an area of our lives still dominated by the old man, we can ask the Holy Spirit to put the old man to death again with respect to that attitude or matter and it shall be done. The Holy Spirit acts as the prosecutor, judge, and executioner in the spiritual realm of the old life.

But He must have our willing cooperation. Not long ago our Siamese cat, Daffy, began to gain weight at an alarming rate. My wife took Daffy to the veterinarian and received a bad diagnosis: most likely a tumor, and at Daffy's age of twelve years the most kind thing to do was to put her to sleep. Naturally it was a disturbing event for the family, and we brought Daffy home for the night to talk it over. The next day we took her back to the vet and asked him to do what we couldn't do—put her to death. It was hard, yet it was the kind and right thing to do. The vet was willing to do the "dirty work," yet we had to give the order. So it is in the spiritual realm; the Holy Spirit will crucify the old man for us, but we must give our consent. Still, if we are not aware of the role of the Spirit in shaping our new and impressionable spiritual lives, we will not call upon Him or submit ourselves to Him. And so our lives in the Spirit will suffer.

Role, Responsibility, and Reality

The interaction of the four factors just discussed influence the *role of the Holy Spirit* in shaping our lives in Christ, the *responsibility of the Christian* to respond to the Spirit, and the *reality of carnal Christians*.

Philippians 2:12-13

Two key verses in the understanding of the shaping of our spiritual life are found in Philippians 2:12-13: "Work out your own salvation with fear and trembling. For it is God which worketh in you both to will and to do of his good pleasure." Paul first urged the Philippians to *work out their salvation*. He was not saying that our salvation is through works; he was simply stressing our legitimate partnership with God in the shaping and maturing of our spiritual lives. We must be willing to allow God to work in our lives. God allows us to be His partners, both in the Christianizing of our own lives and in the evangelization of the world.

Our responsibility for working out our salvation does not leave the security of our soul hanging; it is not the reality of our salvation but its influence upon our own lives that is at stake. The reference in these verses to fear and trembling reflects a healthy reverence for God, an awareness not to take His commands lightly, a sober attitude toward our own weaknesses, and a grasp of the reality of the devil.

The second verse speaks of God's part in the shaping of our lives in Christ. If the Book of Acts had not included a narrative of the Holy Spirit descending to energize the lives of the followers of Christ at Pentecost, we would have been obliged to assume such a happening, so powerful a place does the Spirit occupy in the lives of the believers. For Christian holiness at its foundation is not active, but passive. The Holy Spirit is the source of power, and without Him we are as a glove with no hand within. The Spirit is the sole and absolute judge of what makes up the Christian life. He will never contradict Scripture, but rather illuminate and apply it.

The Role of the Holy Spirit

The Holy Spirit's role in the life of the believer is that of teacher, enabler, judge, prayer partner, umpire, encourager and, perhaps above all, revealer. In soaring words Paul rejoiced, "Eye hath not seen, nor ear heard, neither have entered into the heart of man, the things which God hath prepared for them that love him. But God hath revealed them unto us by his Spirit" (1 Cor. 2:9-10). The Holy Spirit would lead us into a marvelous world not only of reward but also of spiritual maturity.

The Spirit Shapes our Physical Lives

The Holy Spirit seeks to bring our physical lives into submission to God through the reshaping of our minds and hearts. When I am talking with children, especially about trusting Jesus as Lord and Savior, I tell them that when we invite Jesus to come live in our repentant hearts, He comes in with His broom and dustpan, hammer and saw, and begins to sweep and dust and clean up the dark corners of our hearts. I am speaking of the moral change that must accompany our professions of faith, and which is the work of the Holy Spirit in our lives. I tell the children that Jesus is going to build a new person of them from the inside out and that it will take many years and will never be finished until we get to heaven. But every year we should be more like the Master in our personalities and our ways of life.

The Spirit Teaches Us

The Spirit is building a new person from the inside out by teaching the Christian. The Gospel of John sketches a picture of the Spirit giving special guidance and help to the Christian. He guides us into a deepening understanding of spiritual truth (16:13). He reveals to us in the Bible that which shall come to pass both in our individual lives and in the course of the world. (v. 14). He teaches us through our private devotions, through study of the Bible with other Christians, and through the preaching of the Word.

The Spirit also teaches us through hardship and suffering. As we read in Romans 5, our tribulations lead to patient endurance and finally on to hope because the love of God shines in our hearts through the Holy Spirit (vv. 3-5). In Hebrews we see Jesus learning obedience through suffering (4:8). But suffering does not automatically result in a stronger faith and deeper obedience to God—it is a work of the Holy Spirit.

In the Book of Revelation, we learn that when we are "in the Spirit," that is, in a state of mind and heart fixed on God—usually in public worship or private devotion—the Spirit can reveal new truths and interpret the situations of our lives. That was the experience of the writer as he worshiped on the Lord's Day (1:10).

The Spirit is especially involved in the interpretation of Scripture: "And [take] the sword of the Spirit, which is the word of God" (Eph. 6:17). In this admonition Paul spoke of the Spirit using the Word of God to probe the hearts of people. Through the Spirit, the Book becomes "quick [living], and powerful, and sharper than any two-edged sword, piercing even to the dividing asunder of soul and spirit, and of the joints and marrow, and is a discerner of the thoughts and intents of the heart" (Heb. 4:12). Christians should read the Bible in the awareness that it is judging and interacting with our lives and that the Spirit will apply the Word. Is that the way you read the Bible? I hope it may be said of you and me as of an old minister: "He read the Scripture not as if he had written it, but as if listening for a voice."

The Spirit and Our Conscience

The Spirit is also the Lord of our conscience. The word *conscience* simply means "coknowledge," our knowing along with that Someone else who pricks and probes our hearts concerning what is right and wrong, good and evil. While we speak of everyone having a conscience, surely the Christian should have a coknowledge, an agreement with God, concerning moral matters. Conscience, in the lives of those who are estranged from God, may be a negative voice; surely, in the life of the one indwelt by the Spirit, it is an encouraging, positive voice which does not so much warn *against* as it guides *toward* those actions which mark him or her as one of the Father's children. In 1 Corinthians 8, Paul discussed meat offered to idols. While he made no reference to the Spirit in that chapter, he had already made his position clear in the preceding chapter. That chapter speaks of marriage, and after giving his view, Paul concluded, "I think also that I have the Spirit of God" (7:40). The Holy Spirit must dominate the conscience of the Christian, whether the matter under consideration is marriage, meat, or money.

The Spirit and Witnessing

The Holy Spirit desires to empower you and me for more effective witnessing too. The Book of Acts and the various letters of the New Testament are filled with cases of Spirit-led witnessing to individuals and preaching to crowds (Acts 2:4 *f.*; 4:8; 1 Pet. 1:12; 1 Thess. 1:5).

The Spirit Shapes the Church

The work of the Spirit is not limited to the individual Christian, but rather is often at work within the larger church body. One such example of this shaping work is seen in the distribution of spiritual gifts to individual Christians for the building up of the whole church. The Book of Revelation shows us the Spirit's work as giver of the vision and bringer of the message to the churches in chapters 2 and 3. Each of the letters to the seven churches are spoken by the Holy Spirit in the name of Jesus. The same words end each letter: "He that hath an ear, let him hear what the Spirit saith unto the churches" (2:7). The Spirit conveys to your church and mine the will of Jesus through the preaching, the mediation, and the silence.

The Spirit as Bunyan's Interpreter

The role of the Spirit in shaping the life of the willing believer has seldom been expressed more vividly than in Bunyan's *The Pilgrim's Progress*. Bunyan allegorically told of the believer who, on his way to the Celestial City, comes to the house of the Interpreter (the Holy Spirit). The Interpreter first shows Christian a portrait of a man (Jesus) who is the only man authorized to be the believer's guide to the city. Then a parlor full of dust is shown which, when swept, grows more dusty. This is the heart of the unconverted man, filled with original sin; and the uselessness of the law is seen in the broom. But water (the Gospel) is sprinkled on the dust, allowing it to be swept and the parlor made into a fit habitation for a King. Another room reveals two children, Patience and Passion, sitting in chairs. Passion belongs to this world, while Patience is content to wait for the rewards of the next world.

Then Interpreter takes Christian to a wall where a fire burns (God's work of grace in our hearts), although one stands by constantly pouring water upon it (the devil). The other side of the wall reveals a hidden man (Jesus) secretly casting oil (grace) on the fire. Next Christian comes to a beautiful palace, before which stands a great crowd who would go in, having given their name to the one who keeps the book. But the door is guarded by fierce soldiers, and only he who fights bravely can make his way in. From this challenging scene Interpreter leads Christian to a very dark room in which sits a man in an iron cage. Full of despair, he has grieved the Spirit, hardened his heart, and crucified Christ anew.

By this time Christian is anxious to leave, but the Interpreter must show one scene more and takes him into a bedroom where one is rising full of fear and trembling. He has dreamed of judgment and has seen the great throne of God and was not ready. Now Christian may go on his way, as Interpreter asks: "Hast thou considered all these things?"

Christian: "Yes, and they put me in hope and fear."

Interpreter: "Well, keep all things so in thy mind, that they may be as a goad in thy sides to prick thee forward in the way thou must go." So Christian began to gird up his loins and prepare for his journey. Then said the Interpreter, "The Comforter be always with thee, good Christian, to guide thee in the way that leads to the City."[1]

The Responsibility of the Christian

Sometimes we preachers give the impression that salvation consists only of a confession of faith and then, years later, a step from this world into heaven. While these two stages—confession and departure—certainly characterize the dying thief, they are not an adequate model of life in the Spirit! It is significant that Bunyan's famous spiritual classic, second only to the Bible in familiarity to our fathers, was titled *The Pilgrim's Progress*. For between our confession and heaven is a life of struggle and growth which demands our cooperation with the Holy Spirit to be effective.

Even a casual reading of such pivotal passages as Romans 6, Romans 8, and Galatians points up the struggle we continue to have with sin. For by our baptism into Christ's death, our crucifixion with Christ, our dying with Him, we are freed from the *compulsion* of sin but not from the *possibility* of sin.

The Indicatives and the Imperatives

The affirmations, or indicatives in grammar, show that we have been transferred from this present evil age into the kingdom of God's dear Son. Read Romans 6:1-10 and notice the affirmations: We are dead to sin; we were baptized into Christ's death; our old man is crucified with Him; he that is dead is freed from sin; we shall live with Him. Now read verses 11-13. The commands, or imperatives show how we are still threatened by this evil age, passing away but still clutching at us as it reels: Count yourself dead to sin; do not let sin be king; do not yield your body as a tool for sin; yield yourself rather to God. The moral commands *follow* the affirmations because we can only carry out the commands for

holy living through the power of the Holy Spirit. See Ephesians 5:8 and
Colossians 3:1-5 for other examples.

In our spiritual lives, *responsibility* is laid upon us, and *power* is available to carry out that responsibility. This is summed up in Galatians
5:25: "If we live [by] in the Spirit, let us also walk [by] in the Spirit."
The first reference to Spirit means the *power* of the Spirit, while the
second refers to the standard of conduct laid on us by the Spirit. To be
united with Christ in His death means to have His attitude toward sin. To
walk by the Spirit means to accept His power, which is not under our
control, and allow Him to shape our life.

Our Intentional Response

We must make an *intentional* response to the commands of the Spirit
for holy living: an intention to take our hands off our lives, to follow
completely, to allow ourselves to be molded. The biographer of the missionary hero W. W. Borden described Borden's brief career in challenging words: "No reserve, no retreat, no regrets."[2] If we will do the first
two, the third is sure to follow. Yet the first recorded sin in the early
church was a reserve, a holding back of that which belonged to Christ
(Acts 5). Do you fully *intend* as a Christian to give yourself over to the
shaping of Christ through the Spirit?

The active response of Christians to the work of the Spirit in shaping
our lives is twofold: the filling of the Spirit and the taking up of the cross.
It is not possible to take up the cross effectively without the infilling of
the Spirit. The presence of the Spirit is God's gift to every Christian as
one's spiritual birth, but the full power of the Holy Spirit comes only
with full surrender to His guidance. So we hear Paul command the Ephesians: "Be not drunk with wine . . . but be filled with the Spirit" (5:18).
With this filling, or control, of the Spirit comes also the ability and possibility of walking in newness of life: "I can do all things through Christ
which strengtheneth me" (Phil 4:13).

The command to take up our crosses and follow Jesus (Luke 9:23)
stresses that our crucifixion with Christ is a daily, ongoing experience.
To take up our crosses does not mean a willingness to endure the sufferings common to all people—the thorn idea—but rather means to enter
warfare against ourselves! The old man who refuses to die is within us,

as is the power which lusts against the Spirit. The warfare is against the world (which stands for the opposite of the heavenly standard, the "walk according to the Spirit"), the flesh (that within us which loves the world and makes alliance with the devil), and the devil (he who stands in opposition to God). Through the power of the indwelling Spirit, according to our surrender to Him, we can again and again, or more and more, make the great refusal to the devil. The New Testament is full of warnings to be watchful and aware of the dangers of the works of the flesh (Gal. 5:19-26; Phil. 3:17-19; Col. 3:5-7).

The Reality of the Carnal Christian

In relationship to Christ, there are only three kinds of people: *natural men, carnal Christians,* and *spiritual Christians.* The *natural* man is any of us in our unconverted state, living in rebellion toward God. When asked if man is naturally good, Samuel Johnson replied, "No, Madam, no more than a wolf!" The natural man cannot understand the life in Christ: "But the natural man receiveth not the things of the Spirit of God: for they are foolishness unto him: neither can he know them, because they are spiritually discerned" (1 Cor. 2:14).

At the other end of the spiritual spectrum is the *spiritual* man. This person has accepted Jesus as Lord of his life, has been put into a new and saving relationship to God by the Holy Spirit, and is being sanctified in his daily walk of obedience. This is the kind of person you and I *can* be as Christians if we will allow the Spirit to guide us.

In between these extremes is the *carnal* Christian. One of the plainest passages on this matter is 1 Corinthians 3:1-3:

> And I, brethren, could not speak unto you as unto spiritual, but as unto carnal, even as unto babes in Christ. I have fed you with milk, and not with meat: for hitherto ye were not able to bear it, neither yet now are ye able. For ye are yet carnal: for whereas there is among you envying, and strife, and divisions, are ye not carnal, and walk as men?

Notice first of all that these people *were* Christians. The second word in the Greek text of this passage is *brothers.* These folk were "in Christ" even though they were carnal. A carnal, or fleshly, Christian is one whose daily life is controlled not by the Spirit but by self-interests. As

Luther put it, there is in every one of us "that great Pope Self." In the carnal Christian, this self has not been crucified completely or daily.

The Mark of Spiritual Immaturity

In 1 Corinthians 3:1-3, the primary mark of the carnal Christian is seen to be *spiritual immaturity*. These were "babes in Christ" who could not handle spiritual meat but had to have milk. They could not get beyond the basic facts of the gospel in its application in ministry and evangelism (see Heb. 6). In the Corinthian church, baby talk led to jealousy, hurt feelings, and divisions—which are spiritual tantrums. Further, in verse 3 we see that the Christians' life-style had the same appearance to the world as the walk of the lost.

Another picture of *carnal* Christians is seen in Galatians 3:1-3. Paul's words in these verses are strong! These Christians were foolish, unthinking Christians who had been "bewitched" by legalism. Paul bluntly confronted them: "Having begun in the Spirit, are ye now made perfect by the flesh?" Here we see a group of Christians whose grounding in the faith was too shallow; they were easily led off after the innovations of men.

As we look at these two examples of *carnal* Christians, we can see that the people were saved, they were in Christ. The problems arose from their spiritual immaturity; their vulnerability to envy, strife, divisions; their appearing to walk as unsaved in the eyes of the world; their spirit of defeat and lack of joy; and their efforts to live the Christian life by their own energy, apart from the Spirit.

Carnality Hinders the Shaping work of the Spirit Within Us

There are many effective ways to diagram the carnal Christian's life. One of the best diagrams I have seen shows the life of a person seen as a circle with two doors, one at the top and one at the bottom. In the case of the *natural man,* the unsaved man, the door at the top which opens to God is closed, and the door at the bottom, opening to the presence of Satan, is open. In the case of the *spiritual man* the situation is reversed, with the door to God open and the door to Satan closed. The *carnal Christian* is shown as having *both doors opened:* the door leading to God and the door leading to Satan.[3] It is little wonder, then, that so many Christians are spiritually immature, weak, and discouraged. Their hearts are filled with conflicting voices; they are walking civil wars.

How can *carnal Christians,* immature babes in Christ stop being walking civil wars and start on the way to Christian maturity? The answer is simply put in Galatians 2:20: "I am crucified with Christ: nevertheless I live; yet not I, but Christ liveth in me: and the life I now live in the flesh I live by the faith of the Son of God, who loved me, and gave himself for me." We must be willing to allow the Holy Spirit to dominate our thoughts and actions, thus crucifying the old man. We must deepen our sensitivity to the leading of the Spirit through a growing devotional life, which we will examine in our next chapter. We must, through Christian discipline, close the door to Satan's influence.

> Holy Ghost, with light divine,
> Shine upon this heart of mine;
> ....
> Holy Ghost, with power divine,
> Cleanse this guilty heart of mine.
> ....
> Holy Spirit, all divine;
> Dwell within this heart of mine.[4]

Notes

1. John Bunyan, *The Pilgrim's Progress* (New York: The New American Library, Inc., 1964), pp. 33-41.

2. Mrs. Howard Taylor, *Borden of Yale '09* (Philadelphia: China Inland Mission, 1926) p. 260.

3. See diagram of the carnal Christian's life in *Masterlife I: Discipleship Training,* produced by the Church Training Department of The Sunday School Board of the Southern Baptist Convention, 1980, p. 118.

4. Andrew Reed, "Holy Ghost, with Light Divine."

4

The Devotion
Do I Practice the Presence?

> These pages
> are affectionately dedicated
> to that increasing number
> of men and women,
> young and old,
> who are determined,
> with help from above,
> to find God as Reality
> through the practice
> of the Presence.[1]

With those beautiful words, Bishop Ralph Cushman dedicated his excellent devotional book, *Practicing the Presence*. He was right—to find God as reality we must have determination, receive help from above, and practice the Presence. Deep devotional life is not optional for Christians; it is of vital importance. Our devotional life is the gateway to daily fellowship with Christ and a major source of our spiritual power. Yet this is one area in which most Christians fall short primarily because we have not allowed the Holy Spirit enough freedom in shaping our lives and we have allowed the devil too much freedom in obstructing our spiritual lives.

Devotional Life Today

What is meant by *devotional life?* I think one aspect of devotional life is the spiritual disciplines we cultivate such as the reading of the Bible, the time of quiet meditation, the spoken prayers, and the keeping of a devotional journal. The second and wider aspect of the devotional life is the effect the Holy Spirit is allowed to have on our work, our play, and our contacts with other people. Those whose devotional lives are rich have been well described by Samuel Miller, late dean of Harvard's Divinity School:

> In olden days it was said of a certain one that he was a "godly man." We are not accustomed to use the phrase any more, or certainly not as freely as once it was used, but there is something in the phrase that points to one who made himself known to his fellows as a man who dealt with eternal things. He may not have been very rich or very prudent in the ways of the world; he may not have been honored for his achievements or widely known for his name in the newspaper, but the world in which he lived knew that it had within its life one whose vision and wisdom transcended its petty limits.[2]

Reasons for Shallow Devotional Life

Confession is good for the soul, the saying goes, and ought we not confess that the devotional life is sorely lacking in most Christians? The reasons are fairly obvious. First is the increasing secularization of our times. The idolatry with the scientific approach to everything has led to a dividing ￢f life into "religious" and "secular" compartments. In times past, all of life was seen as religious, and in many cultures the religious leaders were the rulers. Now we see one day set aside for religious life, and even that is so often in name only. All this means that our mind-set is not devotional, but secular and materialistic. Tied to our secularism is the modern pace of life. We feel too busy to spend a half hour or an hour each day in quietness and prayer. I confess to having envious thoughts of the preachers of another day who at least had long hours of solitude on horseback, as they made their circuits!

Many thoughtful observers wonder if our society can recover a sense of awareness of God, of a Divine Presence. Our God is an "unknown God" to the modern marketplace. A few days ago I bought a necktie, a nice yellow design. The salesperson approved my choice with the comment: "That's right—that's dressing for power!" To my question he explained—as if to a child—that everyone had read the book on dressing for success and power and that my particular tie was a "power" tie. I just liked it. Equally out of touch with secular thinking was the recent dedication of a new manufacturing plant in a business owned by one of my church families. Four generations of candymakers are known for both their sweet products and the sweetness of their lives and the influence that comes only from a close walk with the Lord. As we dedicated the plant, they reaffirmed the leadership of the Lord and the tenth which would be His.

Materialism, meaninglessness, search for reason to live, breakdown in morals, rising rates of suicide—these characterize our society. And to varying degrees, we are all caught up in it. Would *you* like to experience an added dimension of wholeness and spiritual health? The answer is the Spirit-led devotional life. In the last decade, there has been a growing awareness among theologians that we must build this solid foundation if modern life is to have meaning.

Biblical Models of the Devotional Life

If we wish to cultivate a devotional life, both in daily spiritual disciplines and in the realization of the presence of the Holy Spirit throughout the day, we would benefit from a brief examination of some models from the Bible and from church history.

Old Testament Models

The many facets of rich devotional life can be seen in the lives of Old Testament saints. Enoch walked with God, and "he was not, for God took him" (Gen. 5:24). Sometimes we focus on Enoch's translation from this life to heaven, forgetting his testimony: he pleased God by walking daily with him. In Moses we see more than once the deepest meaning of intercessory prayer, as he pleaded on behalf of the people. The fervency of prayer is seen in Hannah, whom Eli accused of drunkenness. Anyone ever lodged that charge against you while in prayer? The Psalms show us how even a shepherd boy can meditate around his fire and draw lessons from the stars, the sheep, and the dangers of the night. Daniel is a model of discipline as he refused even at the risk of his life to break this thrice daily habit of prayer.

Jesus

The Bible says that Jesus "grew, and waxed strong in spirit, filled with wisdom: and the grace of God was upon him" (Luke 2:40). We also read that "though he were a Son, yet learned he obedience by the things which he suffered" (Heb 5:8) and that He was "in all points tempted like as we are, yet without sin" (Heb. 4:15). I take these verses to mean that the humanity of Jesus was real, not a mask. In His humanity, then, He, too, needed to develop that devotional relationship with the Father by spiritual discipline, through which He gained power for His ministry.

Power for decisions.—The first account we find of our Lord's devotional life is that of the temptation in the wilderness as He faced the great decisions of His ministry (Luke 4:1-13). He experienced a time which apparently included most aspects of the devotional life: solitude, meditation, the study (and quoting) of Scripture, fasting, and while not mentioned specifically, obviously, it was a time of prayer. It was also a time of conflict, of attack by Satan—as our devotional life will be. We must note that Jesus was accompanied by the Holy Spirit and that afterward angels came and ministered to Him. Before choosing the twelve disciples, Jesus spent all night in prayer, laying the decision and the various choices before the Father (Luke 6:12-13).

Power for ministry.—As Jesus began to preach and teach, He would rise while it was still dark and go apart for prayer: "And in the morning, rising up a great while before day, he went out, and departed into a solitary place, and there prayed" (Mark 1:35). The need to draw apart, to be alone, with God is as necessary for you and me as it was for Jesus. Jesus' disciples early realized that the secret of Jesus' power lay in His prayers, and they asked Him to teach them to pray. In the Lord's Prayer and the following teaching on prayer (Matt. 6:6-18; Luke 11:1-13), Jesus spoke of the hidden place of prayer, the manner of prayer, the reward of prayer, and the necessity of forgiveness of our prayers are to be heard. He also gave guidance on the simple but meaningful practice of fasting.

After feeding the five thousand, Jesus withdrew to pray as the day came to a close. George Buttrick described that scene:

> "He went up into a mountain apart to pray: and when the evening was come, he was there alone" (Mt. 14:23). We see him there, a kneeling figure. The red gleam fades. He is silhouetted now against the wheels of stars. The silver wheel slowly turns, but still he kneels. His hands are raised in entreaty. His upturned face catches the dim light. Is he speaking now as if God were on the other side of that ledge of rock? Does the sky ever seem brassy to him, his only answer an echo? What is he saying? We may not know: the place is holy ground.[3]

In that devotional time we call the transfiguration, we see the physical effect of Jesus' prayers, as the unseen world broke in upon this world. We see the communion with the Father that Jesus' prayers brought to daily life. From the mountaintop of devotion, Jesus descended to the valley of need. In the healing of the demonic child and the frustrated powerlessness of the disciples, we see the truth of Jesus' comment, "This kind can come forth by nothing, but by prayer and fasting" (Mark 9:29).

Prayer and intercession.—We find intercession to be prominent in the Master's devotions. At the Last Supper, Jesus revealed that He had been praying for Simon to withstand Satan (Luke 22:31-32). In the high priestly prayer of John 17, Jesus prayed for His followers, both at that time and down through the ages. His request to the Father was for protection for the disciples, for purifying of their lives, for blessing on those who would come to believe in Him, and for our final entrance into heaven. What a model of intercessory prayer. In the garden of Gethsemane, we see Jesus' prayer life taking Him into the Father's presence to find guidance, to lay His will before the Father, and to submit to the cross. There ought be no minimizing of the horrors Jesus felt as He approached the cross. He came from His prayer time filled with the perfect peace of answered prayer. On the cross, we find His final prayer one of forgiveness: "Father, forgive them; they know not what they do" (Luke 23:34).

Victory through prayer.—Jesus often celebrated the victory of faith in His prayers. When the seventy returned victorious in their preaching mission, Jesus rejoiced in the Spirit and thanked God (Luke 10:21). When upon the raising of Lazarus He thanked God for hearing His prayers, He added this note: "And I knew that thou hearest me always" (John 11:42). Jesus' confidence that God heard His prayers came not from His divine knowledge but from His prayer life. In teaching about prayer, Jesus pointed to the essential tie between faith and prayer and assured His followers that God is eager to bless His praying children, including the bestowal of the Holy Spirit in their lives (Mark 11:23-25; Luke 11:1-13; John 14:13-14). In preparation for His return, He bade them watch and pray (Mark 13:33). In the life of our Lord, then, we see the vital place of a devotional life.

Paul

Paul was a man captured by a vision, and he spent his life in obedience to that vision: "Whereupon, O king Agrippa, I was not disobedient to the heavenly vision" (Acts 26:19). That vision of the exalted Christ, that vision of every knee bowed and every tongue confessing was given wings by Paul's devotional life. His solitude in Arabia, his agony for his people Israel, his sometime stern discipline of his churches—were all rooted in his inner life of prayer and meditation and praise. One of the most touching statements of grief-stricken love in the Bible is Paul's prayer for the salvation of Israel (Rom. 9:1-3; 10:1).

Paul's prayers and the Holy Spirit.—First, we see the close relationship of the Holy Spirit and prayer. The Spirit will pray for us when we are too moved or troubled to voice our prayer: "For we know not what we should pray for as we ought: but the Spirit itself maketh intercession for us with groanings which cannot be uttered" (Rom 8:26). The Spirit forms a link between our minds and the mind of God, interceding for us.

Paul's constant attitude of prayer.—We also sense in Paul a constant atmosphere of prayer. This is seen not so much in the account of his journeys in Acts as in his letters to the churches he organized. He assured the churches of his unceasing intercession for them: "Without ceasing I make mention of you always in my prayers." (Rom. 1:9; compare Eph. 1:16; Phil. 1:4; 1 Thess. 1:2; 2 Tim. 1:3).

Paul's prayers and ecstacy.—Paul's devotional life included an element of emotional ecstacy. Indeed, he related in 2 Corinthians 12 an experience of being lifted in his devotions to the "third heaven" (v. 2). Exactly what this meant we do not know, but Paul said that the revelation of his devotional times even posed a threat to his humility and thus led to his thorn in the flesh. Paul also spoke in tongues, which he considered very helpful for his private devotions, but not suited for public worship: "I thank my God, I speak with tongues more than ye all: Yet in the church I had rather speak five words with my understanding, that by my voice I might teach others also, than ten thousand words in an unknown tongue" (1 Cor. 14:18-19). The regular life of private devotion was an essential part of Paul's walk in the Spirit, and he urged his churches to develop such a habit of "unceasing prayer" for both secular leaders and fellow saints.

Models of the Devotional Life from Church History

Augustine: Grace Sufficient

Born in Africa in the middle of the fourth century, Augustine was not only a great leader of the church but perhaps the most human of the saints of the church as well. His *Confessions,* an autobiographical account of his spiritual journey, is a masterpiece of psychological probing of man's heart before God. His lustful and immoral early life is well-known and was poured out in shame in his book. Yet in the midst of his worldliness there was an emptiness that so many others have felt:

> To Thee be praise, glory to Thee, Fountain of mercies. I was becoming more miserable, and Thou nearer. Thy right hand was continually ready to pluck me out of the mire, and to wash me thoroughly, and I knew it not; nor did anything call me back from a yet deeper gulf of carnal pleasures, but the fear of death, and of Thy judgment to come.[4]

We hear Augustine echoed in this poem:

> I sought the Lord, and afterward I knew
> He moved my soul to seek Him, seeking me;
> It was not I that found, O Saviour true,
> No, I was found of Thee.
>
> Thou didst reach forth Thy hand and mine enfold;
> I walked and sank not on the storm-vexed sea,—
> 'Twas not so much that I on Thee took hold,
> As Thou, dear Lord, on me.
>
> I find, I walk, I love, but, O the whole
> Of love is but my answer, Lord, to Thee;
> For Thou wert long before-hand with my soul,
> Always Thou lovedst me.

So it was with Augustine. Like the fleeing man, like the blind man groping along a wall for a door, where there should be a door, must be a door; Augustine was tortured in his heart. In the *Confession,* he likened his life to a ship battered and driven by the winds of passion and greed: "These winds shifted and drove my heart this way and that, time passed on, but I delayed to turn to the Lord; and from day to day deferred to live in Thee, and deferred not daily to die in myself."[6] During this time, Augustine prayed his oft quoted—and honest—prayer: "'Give me chastity and continency, only not yet.' For I feared lest Thou shouldest hear me soon, and soon cure me of the disease of concupiscence which I wished to have satisfied, rather than extinquished."[7]

The supreme spiritual crisis came as Augustine sat weeping in a friend's garden. He turned to the Lord and, in his turning, bore this testimony: "Thou awakest us to delight in Thy praise; for Thou madest us for Thyself, and our heart is restless, til it rest in Thee."[8] In the response of man's heart to God, Augustine has few peers. The *Confessions* are full of Augustine's adoration of God, and a praise poem in book X is a beautifully spiritual "How Do I Love Thee?"[9]

After conversion Augustine renounced all possessions, founded a monastery, and had three quiet years before the Christians of the area insisted he be ordained a priest. At the age of forty-two, he was raised to the office of Bishop of Hippo and served until his death thirty years later. He agreed to be consecrated a bishop only if certain days each week were left free for prayer and meditation. That didn't work out but does give us Augustine's understanding of the importance of a devotional life. In *The City of God,* he commented, "No man has a right to be so immersed in active life as to neglect the contemplation of God."

The *Confessions* is full of prayers asking God to enlarge Augustine's soul, to fill his spiritual hunger, to forgive the time wasted in riotous living. In his confessions, we see ourselves in our own spiritual journey. We see a man overwhelmed by the wideness of God's mercy and the richness of Divine fellowship. The Lord was food, family, fame, fellowship, and freedom. From his first day of conversion until he lay on his deathbed, his plea to God was, "Narrow is the mansion of my soul; enlarge thou it, that Thou mayest enter in. It is ruinous; repair Thou it."[10] Only the Holy Spirit can call a man away from sin, lead him to the light, and fill and enlarge his soul to be a fit mansion for the Lord. Augustine left a shining record of the devotional life that proves what the Holy Spirit can do even in a pre-Christian life of such immorality.

Francis: Poverty Embraced

Of all the medieval saints, the most familiar and beloved is Francis of Assisi (1182-1226). He was from a wealthy Italian family. As a young man, he wandered in search of purpose in his life. While praying one day, he felt the Man on the crucifix above him was calling him to a new way of life, a life of poverty. This charge led him to renounce his family and their wealth—he stripped off his clothes before his father and the Bishop of Assisi and declared his commitment to God alone. Gathering about him a few followers, he received the blessing of Rome, and so began the "penitents of Assisi."

Many wonderful stories can be told about Francis, some of which sound strange to modern ears. We are all familiar with the story of his preaching to the birds. The account has it that, while preaching to a crowd, he had bidden the twittering birds to keep silent while he talked. After he finished the sermon for people, he soon passed a large flock of birds in a tree who flew down and listened attentively as he preached to them. The content? We must praise God for all His gifts! The truth of the legend surely lies in the humility and gratitude of Francis for all God's creation.

The story of Francis's first wandering companion, told in *The Little Flowers of St. Francis,* sheds light on his devotional life. For a while after Francis's renunciation of the world, those who knew him felt him crazy; he was scoffed at and despised, the target of mud and stones. But a wealthy noble of Assisi named Bernard began to ponder Francis's ways. He invited him to supper one evening and then invited him to pass the night as a guest. Bernard had a second bed put in his own bedroom, and a lamp burned all night. Francis went to bed as soon as he entered the room, so as not to appear overly sanctimonious, and pretended to drop off to sleep immediately. Bernard soon followed him to bed and pretended to snore. Francis, thinking his host sound asleep, then arose and began to pray, raising his hands and eyes to heaven with the soft cry, "My God! My God!" and weeping. He stayed on his knees all night, repeating over and over that one phrase. Bernard was so touched by Francis' devotions and by the obvious presence of the Spirit that he resolved that, come daylight, he would follow Christ with Francis.

One day, Francis saw a vision of an angel playing a viol. Francis began singing about his Lord. His singing would often end in tears as he contemplated Christ. Then with repeated sighs and groanings, this holy man would lift his hands to heaven. Francis was, indeed, a man who desired that his entire life be a sweet music to the Lord. Apparently oblivious to materialism, to pride, to self—his life gave the Church pause too. The pope said to Francis and his first band of followers: "My dear sons, your life appears most hard and rude to us; although we believe your fervor to be so great that we have no doubt."

Francis's greatest compliment has been the attributing of the stigmata, the prints of the wounds of Jesus in his own flesh. He also seems to have developed the habit of often passing entire nights in prayer. On one occasion, he was found by a disciple praying in a solitary place, kneeling with hands and face lifted toward heaven, saying, "Who are Thou, my dearest Lord? And who am I, a most vile worm and Thy most unprofitable servant?" As his follower watched and lifted his eyes, too, to heaven he saw a great torch of fire which appeared to light on Francis' head, and a voice which spoke to him. Soon after this experience, Francis received the marks of crucifixion in his hands, feet, and side.[11] These he reluctantly showed to his followers when he could no longer hide them. Again, the ultimate meaning of the stigmata is that those around Francis saw in him a life which was Christlike.

The same idea of walking in the Spirit of Jesus is seen in a vision experienced by one of Francis's followers. The vision was of a wonderful procession of apostles and martyrs led by the virgin, all walking very carefully with heads down and staring at the ground earnestly, seeking to follow in the very steps of Christ. At the end of this magnificent procession was Francis, lagging behind, barefoot, and wearing a shabby brown robe; he alone, the "Troubadour of Christ," the "Bridegroom of Lady Poverty," was walking easily and surely in Jesus's steps. What a beautiful example of the inner devotional life shining through to glorify God!

Theresa: Ecstatic Meditation

In the Church of Santa Maria della Vittoria in Rome may be seen Bernini's most famous sculpture, *Saint Theresa in Ecstasy*. It is a moving baroque work, and Bernini was able to convey in marble the texture of flesh, silk, feathers, and even clouds. The work shows the famous vision of Theresa of Avila—that of an angel coming to thrust a lance into her heart, symbolizing her rapture in spiritual devotion to Christ. In her visions, which gradually came to accompany her devotions, she said she could see Christ exactly as He was painted by the artists, rising from His sepulcher.

Like so many deeply spiritual Christians, Theresa (1515-1582) did not start out that way! A girl of the aristocratic class, she became a nun at nineteen. But by her own confession, she was not a prayerful, spiritual person. When she was forty, her deeper life began to bloom. As she said, it was then that her "prayer began to be solid like a house." Five years before her death, she wrote *The Interior Castle,* a full and systematic account of the inner devotional life. This work teaches the gradual unfolding of our spiritual growth and power under the image of rooms which the key of prayer unlocks:

> While I was beseeching the Lord today that He would speak through me . . . I began to think of the soul as if it were a castle made of single diamond or of very clear crystal, in which there are many rooms, just as in heaven there are many mansions.[12]

A little later she spoke again of the secret of her spiritual life as the entering in of this castle:

> Now let us return to our beautiful and delightful castle and see how we can enter it. I seem rather to be talking nonsense, . . . For we ourselves are the castle; and it would be absurd to tell someone to enter a room where he was in it already! . . . You will have read certain books on prayer which advise the soul to enter within itself: and that is exactly what this means . . . As far as I can understand, the door of entry into this castle is prayer and mediation.[13]

Theresa's early religious life, like many of ours, reveals an acquaintance with the reality of what has been called "spiritual gravity," the pull of this world on the soul. Her later life is an example of the life "pierced by God's love."

Theresa was known for her heights of ecstatic meditation. She experienced a long series of visions and voices which would sometimes come upon her in public, to her great distress. Her writings reveal her frank suspicions of the source of these visions and her efforts to avoid delusions by the devil. She is a classic example of the flowering of the spiritual life to bloom not in inner contemplation only but in active ministry and work for God. She said the entire point of her inner union with God was "Work! Work! Work!" Her prayers and visions gave her strength and power to carry out her journeys as founder and reformer of religious groups. Her word to her pupils and to us:

> What is the good, my daughters, of being deeply recollected in solitude, and multiplying acts of love, and promising our Lord to do wonders in His service, if, when we come out of our prayer, the least thing makes us do the exact opposite? . . . If, as David says, one becomes holy with the holy, who can doubt that this soul, who is now become *one thing* with the

Mighty God by his high union of spirit with Spirit, shares His strength? It is hence that the saints have drawn that courage which made them capable of suffering and dying for their God.[14]

While much of Theresa's experience and teaching about the deeper life of the soul is hard to understand, we have no problem grasping the wonderful truths in the following lines written in her manual of worship. I found a beautiful hand-lettered copy of these words in an old book years ago and only recently realized their source:

> Let nothing disturb thee,
> Nothing affright thee;
> All things are passing;
> God never changeth;
> Patient endurance
> Attaineth to all things;
> Who God possesseth
> In nothing is wanting;
> Alone God sufficeth.

Brother Lawrence: God Is Everywhere

This man did nothing more sensational than turning his monastery kitchen into God's throne room for forty years. Lawrence's real name was Nicholas Herman (c. 1605-1691), first a soldier who was made lame in battle, then a servant to a wealthy man, and finally a cook for the rest of his life. He is known for his clumsiness too. We know him and his spiritual depth through a dozen or so letters he wrote to friends and four conversations he had with a visitor.[15] The phrase "practicing the Presence" is his, and he strongly felt we "should establish ourselves in a sense of God's Presence, by continually conversing with Him." He admitted that "in order to form a habit of conversing with God continually, and referring all we do to Him, we must first apply to Him with some diligence: but that after a little care we should find His love inwardly excites us to it without any difficulty."[16]

Concerning Christian character and duty, Lawrence often told God, "Lord, I cannot do this unless Thou enablest me," and God's Spirit provided strength. Likewise, when he fell short of a proper walk in the Spirit, he would pray, "I shall never do otherwise if you leave me to myself; 'tis You must hinder my failing and mend what is amiss."[17] After this he did not worry. And such an attitude of close walk developed only at the end of four years' doubting of his salvation, in which time he was tormented by the conviction that he was damned. He finally thought it through like this: "I engaged in a religious life only for the love of God, and I have endeavored to act only for Him; whatever becomes of me, whether I be lost or saved, I will always continue to act purely for the love of God. I shall have this good at least, that til death I shall have done all this is in me to love Him."[18]

Lawrence made no distinction between special prayer times and the work he did washing pots and pans. In one of the conversations, he said, "The time of business does not differ with me from the time of prayer; and in the noise and clutter of my kitchen, while several persons are at the same time calling for different things, I possess God in as great tranquaillity as if I were upon my knees at the Blessed Sacrament."[19] Concerning set times of prayer, he said, "Sometimes I consider myself as a stone before a carver, whereof he is to make a statue: presenting myself thus before God, I desire Him to make His perfect image in my soul."[20] In order to practice the presence of God, which by the Spirit can transform our very ordinary lives, we must still heed the words Brother Lawrence penned nearly three hundred years ago: "I know that for the right practice of it the heart must be empty of all other things, because God will possess the heart alone."[21] Every Christian desiring a deeper walk with Christ would do well to read *The Practice of the Presence of God* often.

George Muller: Reality of Prayer

One morning George Muller had already been in prayer for two hours, enjoying the Lord and thinking Him for a miracle which Muller felt confident was on the way. That morning, unless God intervened, the four hundred orphans who were at that very moment gathering in the orphanage dinning hall would find no milk in their mugs—not a drop. God had never failed to provide the needs of that ministry of faith; and so it was that, while the mugs were still empty, Muller led the children in the blessing, thanking God for food—and milk! As he finished praying, a loud knock at the door was heard, and there stood a milkman! "Mr. Muller, I don't know how it happened, but my milk wagon broke down right out front here. The wheel is smashed; I cannot get the load of milk to town—it's all yours!"[22]

As a young man, George Muller (1805-1898) came to England from Germany in the early eighteen hundreds, with a burning desire to serve Christ with his whole life. He developed, as part of his ministry, five great orphanages in Bristol. He never asked anyone for help; he never went into debt; he acted out of faith day by day. By his death, he had received and used over seven and one-half million dollars! He often admitted that he found it was as hard to trust God for a shilling at the start as it was for a thousand pounds in later life. The more he exercised his spiritual life, the more it grew. Muller kept a record of over fifty thousand answered prayers and delighted in the Lord when each answer came! God was Muller's only source for the financial needs of his vast ministry, and that resource was sufficient.

We are obliged to ask ourselves if our devotional lives receive the attention from us that Muller gave to his spiritual walk. As Muller wrote in his book,

> The joy which answers to prayer give, cannot be described; and the impetus which they afford to the spiritual life is exceedingly great. The experience of his happiness I desire for all my Christian readers. If you believe indeed in the Lord Jesus for the salvation of your soul, if you walk uprightly and not regard iniquity in your heart, if you continue to wait patiently, and believingly upon God; then answers will surely be given to your prayers.[23]

Thomas Kelly: Authentic Presence

Of Quaker heritage, Thomas Kelly (1893-1941) had the advantage of a spiritually oriented life. As a college student, he came under the Christlike spell of the Quaker mystic, Rufus Jones. The First World War interferred with Kelly's dream of missionary work, and he decided to prepare himself for a teaching career in philosophy. He taught at Earlham College, the University of Hawaii, and Haverford College.

As a young adult, Kelly pursued fame and was spiritually restless. Then, in 1937, only four or five years before his death, a change came about. How or why, no one knows. But the strain and striving left his life and was replaced by an authentic presence of Jesus. In a series of lectures, he began to say,

To you in this room who are seekers, to you, young and old who have toiled all night and caught nothing, but who want to launch out into the deep and let down your nets for a draught, I want to speak as simply, as tenderly, as clearly as I can. For God *can* be found. There *is* a last rock for your souls, a resting place of absolute peace and joy and power and radiance and security.[24]

He began to speak less as one who had *knowledge about* and more as one who enjoyed *acquaintance with* the Lord. He wrote to Rufus Jones, "The reality of the Presence has been very great at times recently. One knows at first hand what the old inquiry meant, 'Has Truth been advancing among you?'"[25] A collegue said of the deeper life Kelly had found, "He almost startled me, and he shocked some of us who were still walking in the ways of logic and science and flesh, by the high areas of being he had penetrated."[26] This practicing of the Presence brought with it a growing reemphasis on the central place of devotion in the Christian's life. Nine days before he died, Kelly sent a letter to a friend in which he mentioned a manuscript he was working on, dealing with the practical procedure and spiritual walk of one who is living by, and turning toward, the Light within, both in public worship and private devotion.

Thomas Kelly died suddenly of a heart attack at the age of forty-seven. In *A Testament of Devotion,* he left us the record of the spiritual journey of a twentieth-century man, able to live both in and above this world. As he said,

How, then, shall we lay hold of that Life and Power, and live the Life of prayer without ceasing? By quiet, persistent practice in turning of all our being, day and night, in prayer and inward worship and surrender, toward Him who calls in the deeps of our souls. An inner, secret turning to God can be made fairly steady, after weeks and months and years of practice and lapses and failures and returns. Begin now, as you read these words, as you sit in your chair, to offer your whole selves, utterly and in joyful abandon, in quiet, glad surrender to Him who is within.[27]

Practice the Presence

What do these folk, genuinely human but towering spiritually over most of us, have to say to you and me in our understanding of the devotional life in the Spirit? Augustine showed us that God is seeking us even as we think we seek Him. Christ wants not only to forgive, cleanse, and fill the unsaved; He will perform the same works of grace in the heart of the Christian who seeks a deeper inner life. The beautiful spirit of love and gratitude seen in Augustine commends itself to every believer. Francis showed us that longing for identification with Christ which should fill each Christian's heart and the power of the life modeled after Christ.

Theresa's experience tells us what we have already experienced—the earth has a spiritual pull downward, which only the interior life can break. Her spiritual journey inward to find the deep joy of union with Christ, and then the outward journey expressing that joy in service, is a benediction upon us all. And Lawrence—God is wherever His children are; He was not ashamed to visit Lawrence amid pots and pans. Do everything as unto God. Thomas Kelly lived in no monastery, nor was he a formal religious leader. But passing by us, he showed us how it is possible, in our time, to practice the Presence.

Notes

1. Ralph S. Cushman, *Practicing the Presence* (Nashville: Abingdon Press, 1936), p. 5.

2. Samuel Miller, *The Life of the Soul* (Waco: Word Books, 1951), pp. 78-79.

3. George Buttrick, *Prayer* (Nashville: Abingdon Press, 1942), p. 30.

4. Augustine, *The Confessions of Saint Augustine,* Cardinal edition Edward B. Pusey, trans. (New York: Cardinal Press, 1952), p. 10.

5. Author unknown, "I Sought the Lord."

6. Augustine, p. 99.

7. Ibid., p. 140.

8. Ibid., p. 1.

9. Ibid., p. 177.

10. Ibid., p. 3.

11. Francesco d'Assisi, *"The Little Flowers" and the Life of St. Francis with the "Mirror of Perfection,"* Thomas Okey, trans. (New York: E. P. Dutton and Co., 1910), pp. 110-111.

12. Theresa, *The Interior Castle,* E. Allison, trans. (Garden City: Doubleday Image Books, 1961), p. 105.

13. Ibid., p. 31.

14. Quoted in Evelyn Underhill, *Mystics of the Church*, pp. 180-81.

15. Brother Lawrence, *Practicing the Presence of God,* Hugh Martin, ed. (London: SCM Press, 1956).

16. Ibid., p. 12.

17. Ibid.

18. Ibid., p. 11.

19. Ibid., p. 22.

20. Ibid., p. 28.

21. Ibid., p. 33.

22. Ann Talbott McPherson, *They Dared to Be Different* (Chicago: Moody Press, 1967), p. 171-172.

23. George Muller, *Answers to Prayer* (Chicago: Moody Press, n.d.), p. 66.

24. Thomas R. Kelly, *A Testament of Devotion,* p. 18.

25. Ibid., p. 19.

26. Ibid., p. 24.

27. Ibid., p. 38.

5

The Deeper Life
How Can I Deepen
My Devotional Life?

The devotional life of quietness, meditation, and prayer is vital in the Christian's life. Sometimes, as we struggle to develop holy habits, the devil would have us think that we are frantically fanning a fire, vainly trying to keep the devotional flame going. But that is not at all true; rather, in our devotional lives, we are keeping in touch with a great spiritual fire which, through the Holy Spirit, is already flaming in this world! Our individual lives will become as dying embers raked out of the fire if the devil has his way!

Images of Devotional Life

Paul spoke in Ephesians 3:17-18 of his prayer "That Christ may dwell in your hearts by faith; that ye, being rooted and grounded in love, May be able to comprehend with all saints what is the breadth, and length, and depth, and height." By "rooted and grounded," he surely referred to devotional life under the guidance of the Spirit as the root system of a flourishing spiritual life. Our interior lives of devotion feed and expand our desire for God. As we meet Him in an increasingly personal way, we have a growing awareness of His presence and guidance and power. As Underhill pointed out, only as our private devotion feed and expand our lives can we be capable of "being to the Eternal Goodness what his own hand is to a man—a supple and living tool."[1]

Paul also spoke of our lives as the dwelling place of the Holy Spirit. Only by deepening our devotional lives can our souls be, as Theresa called it, interior castles. If we are shallow in spirit, our souls—and our Lord—must dwell in shacks! Our devotional lives are stairways, to use another image, leading to the audience chamber of the great King. As the writer of Hebrews graphically described, our entrance into the holiest of all places is through the blood of Christ. We dare not come before Him in a sloven spirit. Our souls take their garments from our devotional lives; how strange it must appear to God for us to appear before Him in rags.

Yet, whether we speak of the devotional life under the images of fire, root, hand, castle, stairway, or garment—the key to development of the inner life is a desire.

A Desire for Devotion

Without a desire to practice the Presence, our lives cannot grow or be pleasing to God. Thomas Kelly expressed the challenge so well:

> Let me talk very intimately and very earnestly with you about Him who is dearer than life. Do you really want to live your lives, every moment of your lives, in His Presence? Do you long for Him, crave Him? Do you love His Presence? Does every drop of blood in your body love Him? Does every breath you draw breathe a prayer, a praise to Him? Do you sing and dance within your selves, as you glory in His love? Have you set your-selves to be His, and *only* His, walking every moment in holy obedience? I know I'm talking like an old-time evangelist. But I can't help that, nor dare I restrain myself and get prim and conventional. We have too long been prim and restrained. The fires of the love of God, of our love toward God, and of His love toward us, are very hot. "Thou shalt love the Lord thy God with all thy heart and soul and mind and strength." Do we really do it? Is love steadfastly directed toward God, in our minds, all day long? Do we intersperse our work with gentle prayers and praises to Him? Do we live in the steady peace of God, a peace down at the very depths of our souls, where all strain is gone and God is already victor over the world, already victor over our weaknesses?[2]

Every Christian a Mystic?

> O the pure delight of a single hour
> That before thy throne I spend;
> When I kneel in pray'r, and with thee, my God
> I commune as friend with friend![3]

Why, Fanny Crosby talked as if an hour spent in meditation and prayer were a small thing! Have you *ever* spent a solid hour in constant medita-tion and prayer? As a part of a discipleship training program, a group in my church recently spent *three* hours in silent meditation and prayer.

Every person admitted being apprehensive at the start of the period and strangely changed at the end! But what about the people given as examples in the last chapter—did they pray long periods of time, and were they spiritual freaks? Were these ordinary people like you and me who merely opened more of themselves to God? Were they mystics? Is mysticism only for the few?

While some would make a distinction between mysticism and the ordinary experience of most Christians, I feel that is an arbitrary division. Allowing for the fact that some of the great spiritual guides of the church, such as Theresa of Avila, were of a highly emotional nature, the Christian mystic

> is one for whom God and Christ are not merely objects of belief, but living facts experimentally known at first-hand; and mysticism for him becomes, in so far as he responds to its demands, a life based on this conscious communion with God. When St. Augustine said, 'My life shall be a real life, being wholly full of Thee,' he described the ideal of a true Christian mysticism.[4]

Mysticism is not to be associated with astrology, fortune-telling, soothsaying, seances, or mental telepathy. It is not supernatural in the sense of the occult. While there is mystery about mysticism, it is the divine mystery of the presence of God in our lives; it is religion in its deepest and most inward level. *Mysticism is simply the conscious practice of the presence of God in our everyday life.*

Such experiences as Abraham had as he offered Isaac, Moses at the burning bush, and Jesus on the mount of transfiguration are mystical encounters with God. As Wayne Oates aptly puts it, "the place to look for being laid hold of by the spirit of mystical experience is in the serendipitous breakthroughs of the Eternal into the commonplace, the routine, and even the drudgery of daily existence."[5] Simply to contemplate the goodness of God in our own lives should make our devotional time fairly glow with His grace.

In daily devotional communion, rather than the exceptional sense of the rapture, every Christian should be a true mystic. The "mystic way" is usually defined as having three strands which should be unfolding the life of every Spirit-led Christian: the moral struggles and purging which are part of the putting to death of the old man; the continually developing life of prayer and its accompanying sweetness; and the growing sense of union with Christ—"nevertheless I live, yet not I but Christ liveth in me." It is easy to see these strands in Paul's life.

> Jesus, Thou Joy of loving hearts,
> Thou Fount of life, Thou light of men,
> From the best bliss that earth imparts,
> We turn, unfilled, to Thee again.
> ....
> Our restless spirits yearn for Thee,
> Where'er our changeful lot is cast;
> Glad when Thy gracious smile we see,
> Blest when our faith can hold Thee fast.
> O Jesus, ever with us stay,
> Make all our moments calm and bright;
> Chase the dark night of sin away,
> Shed o'er the world Thy holy light.[6]

Elements of the Devotional Life

A devotional life must be tailored to fit the individual's personality, emotional makeup, stage of Christian walk, and daily schedule. Some of us are introverts and some are extroverts, some are reflective and some are activists. No single path of spiritual devotion fits all of us, so you must design your own. However you design your personal plan, it ought to include as parts of devotion the gaining of a proper *spiritual attitude* of devotion, nourishing *spiritual food* which leads to communion with God, *spiritual habits* and aids to further our development, and responsible *spiritual work*.

The following elements of devotion help accomplish these objectives: silence, meditation, spoken prayer, Scripture, a spiritual journal, dreams, fasting, and simplicity of life. For the most part, we control these elements of devotion. There is, of course, the role of the Spirit which we will talk about a bit later.

Silence

Kipling spoke of the sun coming up "like thunder" in its silent bursting on the scene. Silence is powerful. Our trouble is that we are afraid of silence—we have almost become a culture devoid of silence. We wake to radios, go to sleep by TV, and even exercise to music. But our interior lives need a certain amount of silence, like flowers need the sun. Silence is a doorway into our spiritual houses. So as we come to the devotional time each day, let us begin by simply becoming quiet.

Select a place which can be used regularly and identified with the devotional life. Notice the clock ticking, the bird singing on the limb outside, the beating of your heart. Take care not to drop off to sleep. After the surface images have flitted around your mind till they are tired, you may want to write a spiritual journal. Silence is needful to calm our minds and hearts, and will also prove vital as a part of the actual prayer period.

Meditation

Meditation is the "in thing" these days. From the Eastern religions has come to our culture a new sense of the value of spiritual meditation. From Hare Krishna chanting to the incense-filled atmosphere of Zen Buddhism, meditation is on the scene. But would you be able to answer if a Christian friend asked you, "How do I go about Christian meditation?" Perhaps not since we have put little value on this practice. Yet meditation has value for our devotional lives because it helps us go deeper and prepare for active prayer.

Religious art.—You may find it helpful to use symbolism, art, music, spiritual classics, and Scripture in meditation. Some folk gaze upon an empty cross and think upon the resurrection. Other symbols, such as the dove, the flame, and the fish, can aid in quiet meditation. Meditating upon the meaning of favorite religious paintings can be helpful. Hunt's [*Christ*] *The Light of the World* and Hofman's *Christ in Gethsemane*, along with works of the masters like Rembrandt's *Denial of Peter* and the *Return of the Prodigal* have been sources of inner strength in meditation to many. You could keep a book of great religious art, such as *The Bible and Its Painters,*[7] at hand, or put a favorite work where you will see it often during the day and be able to think upon it

Hymns and prayers.—Religious music can be a valuable aid in meditation, especially the pondering of the words of great hymns. The Christian hymnal could well be, next to the Bible, the major book at hand in this special period of the day. Along with the deep thoughts and prayers expressed in the hymns by the saints through the years, add those which have been a part of your own spiritual pilgrimage.

I find it helpful during my meditation period to read prayers of fellow pilgrims; it somehow tunes my heart to sing His praise. Great collections of prayers may easily be found; among those which have been most helpful to many pilgrims are John Baillie's *A Diary of Private Prayer* and a book long out of print, *Lancelot Andrewes and His Private Devotions*. You may also want to read the great classics of the spiritual pilgrimage, such as Augustine's *Confessions,* Kelly's *A Testament of Devotion,* and Brother Lawrence's *The Practice of the Presence of God.*

Pitfalls of meditation.—Unfortunately some common pitfalls exist concerning meditation and devotional life in general. First, we must beware of the spiritual folly of saying to ourselves, "I'm doing something special and deep; I'll bet my friends aren't this spiritual!" Well, we aren't either, and the sin of pride just crept back in! We develop our inner lives because we hunger for closeness with God and because the Holy Spirit brings us to this time of blessed communion which feeds our souls. Second, we are mistaken to expect some great spiritual light to envelop us in meditation or other aspects of devotion, or some deep thrill or sweetness. All great leaders of the inner life testify to much ordinariness and the need to keep determinedly plodding on, until there is, indeed, the Presence.

Prayer

A definition.—Not all prayer is spoken prayer, nor must prayer even be consciously framed sentences. And the silence which ought to be a part of this prayer element of our devotional time is true prayer too. As Samuel Miller said, "The words of a prayer depend for their meaning on the silences of prayer, and if there are no silences we can well be sure that there is no meaning to the words."[8] So what is prayer? "It is . . . a deliberate act of our whole being to make real to ourselves the Divine Reality."[9] "Prayer, if it is real, is an acknowledgement of our finitude, our need, our openness to be changed, our readiness to be surprised, yes astonished by the beams of love."[10]

Hindrances of prayer.—But it is not easy to develop this period of conscious prayer. The old man in us fights it, tooth and nail. The hindrances are legion and of all natures. One cannot pray because he has suffered, another because he has doubts about prayers being answered, another has simply grown cold in spirit

In another category are those hindrances due to willful sin and disobedience. Barriers to prayer are thrown up by unforgiveness and unchristian attitudes. Hebrews 10:22 admonishes us to "draw near with a true heart in full assurance of faith, having our hearts sprinkled from an evil conscience, and our bodies washed with pure water." That verse indicates that there can be no deceit or insincerity or doubt which overwhelms assurance, no deliberate sin but rather a cleansed heart when we come to pray. Likewise we remember the admonition in 1 Peter 3:7 given to husbands: "Likewise, ye husbands, dwell with them according to knowledge, giving honour unto the wife, as unto the weaker vessel, and as being heirs together of the grace of life; *that your prayers not be hindered*" [author's italics]. Taking these verses seriously would remove many hindrances to prayer.

Hindrances of another nature include lack of privacy or comfort. It is true that we can condition ourselves to pray in various situations—a recent survey of ministers showed they prayed in the office (42 percent), home (20 percent), anywhere quiet (12 percent), church (10 percent), car (8 percent), walking (5 percent), and jogging (3 percent).[11] However, you need to pray where you feel quiet and undisturbed. We tend to identify certain rooms or pieces of furniture with certain activities, and this is so with a place for devotion. Some people pray best while kneeling, others sitting, standing, or while walking. The active mind can be a distraction when everything from the forgotten chore to the shirt which needs to be taken to the laundry camps on your mental doorstep. Try writing down these intruders of the prayer time so you can deal with them later. Other matters which stubbornly refuse to go away or slip through the mind's door may be sent by God for your attention, so, likewise, jot them down.

Deepening steps of prayer.—There are many approaches to voicing different kinds of prayer concerns. Some Christians organize prayer in the form of a house of prayer. Theresa, for example, did this in the *Interior Castle*. Evelyn Underhill in *The House of the Soul* spoke of an upper story which is our capacity for God, a lower story which comprises our daily cares, and a basement of natural life and instincts.[12] She used the Lord's Prayer to begin at the watchtower of faith and work her way to the lower levels of the house of prayer.

Leslie Weatherhead, in *A Private House of Prayer,* said he devised a method of prayer during his many travels.[13] He pondered Jesus' words: "When thou prayest, enter into thy closet, and when thou hast shut thy door, pray to thy Father which is in secret" (Matt. 6:6), and concluded Jesus was referring to an imaginative room. The prayer house model Weatherhead recommended has seven rooms: room one, where we affirm the presence of God; room two, where God is praised, thanked, and adored; room three, dark upon entrance but growing lighter as we move to the window, is the place of confession, forgiveness, and unloading. Room four is set aside for affirmation of the sinner by God and our reception of His love; room five is the room for purified desire and sincere petition. Room six is that of intercession for others; and room seven is a big room at the top set aside for meditation.

However we design our houses of prayer, or if we use an acrostic such as ACTS, we need to deal with the common ventures of prayer: *adoration, confession, thanksgiving,* and *supplication.* Spiritual honesty compels us to find place as well for our feelings of anger, grief, and doubt.

Adoration may follow the lines of the psalms, or spring from contemplation of nature. Many hymns are prayers of adoration. Also, though we are dealing with regular habit of definite devotional time, our prayers should naturally rise throughout the day. Ancient Christian tradition speaks of the "Jesus Prayer," or the "Prayer of Aspiration." Francis of Assissi is said to have spent all night saying over and over, "My God and All! What art Thou? And What am I?" This is akin to the psalmist's cry, "Whom have I in heaven but Thee?" Such brief snatches of scriptural adoration are suggested by many spiritual guides to be said over and over throughout the day until it becomes an unconscious turning toward God. George Buttrick suggests punctuating our day by ejaculatory prayers— the word *jacula* means spear, and we should have spears of adoration throughout the day.[14]

Confession is to prayer what bathing is to a person's daily life. The Bible emphasizes two things about this aspect of prayer: All persons sin and therefore need confession, and God is ready and willing to forgive if we confess our sins (1 John 1:9). The neglect of this aspect of prayer will absolutely wither all other aspects. One cannot approach that eternal light where God alone dwells if known sin is unconfessed. We may stand at the door and look in, but unforgiven and hidden sin cannot go within His throne room. Yet God does not require perfection, but confession.

Confession was an area well known by Lancelot Andrewes, dean of Westminster, a leading scholar among those who translated the King James Version of the Bible. He sold himself to be the court favorite of James the First. Caught like a moth circling the flame, Andrewes came to approve the immoral doings of the court. His friends knew it, God knew it, he knew it—and as biographer Alexander Whyte puts it, "Bishop Andrewes's soul is still in hell to the end of his life, and a hundred times in his remorseful *Devotions,* because he did it." Yet Whyte's appreciation of the inner life of Andrewes led him to say "But, absolutely and utterly believing that Andrewes means all that he says when he is on his knees clothed in sackcloth and with dust on his head and a rope around his neck, I am not afraid at the worst thing that I meet with in his previous life."[15] "O God," said Andrewes every night in secret, "save me from making a god of the king." In Andrewes's *Private Devotions,* never intended for public eye, we see his confessions to God:

> Behold me, O Lord, behold me, the greatest, the worst, the most wretched of sinners. And what shall I now say, or in what shall I open my mouth? What shall I answer, when I am guilty, guilty, guilty? I will go over my sins unto Thee in the bitterness of my soul; O that it may be in its bitterest bitterness! . . . I have sinned against Thee, most often and grievously have I sinned against Thee.
> . . . .
> That I should thus, for leeks and garlick, have left the bread of angels: that I should thus, for the husks of swine, have despised my Father's table: O wretched, frenzied me! Who bewitched me to such foolishness?
> . . . .
> After so many backslidings, with what confidence can I now return? With none. Altogether confused, altogether covered with confusion, I walk, I sit, I lie down. . . . I then, trusting in Thy mercy, that forgiveth at the least seventy times seven, stand afar off; and lowlily, as I ought, and most humbly smiting upon my breast, say and repeat, again and again, God have mercy on me a sinner, on me a most wretched sinner . . . O Thou to Whom prayer can never be made without a hope of pardon.[16]

Thanksgiving is necessary for God's people. We should readily offer thanksgiving as we reflect upon our own lives, our many rescues, and that great salvation God has given us. Our thanksgiving is really a confession of our faith and confidence in our Heavenly Father. More thanksgiving would lead to more rest and peace and tranquillity for our souls. We must cultivate thankful hearts by voicing our gratitude to God. Sometimes we get too busy to thank God. When I think I'm that busy, I remember how astronaut Gordon Cooper prayed a moving prayer of thanksgiving as he orbited the earth in his spacecraft on May 22, 1963:

> Father, thank You, especially for letting me fly this flight. Thank You for the privilege of being able to be in this position; to be up in this wondrous place, seeing all these many startling, wonderful things that You have created. Help guide and direct all of us that we may shape our lives to be much better Christians, trying to help one another. Help us to complete this mission successfully. Help us in our future space endeavors that we may show the world that a democracy really can compete, and still are able to do things in a big way, and are able to do research, development, and can conduct many scientific and very technical programs. We ask in Thy name. Amen.

Petitions or supplication to the Father is the element of prayer we use most often, and that speaks of our need for a more mature faith. Yet, there is a definite place for petitions, concerning both our own needs and those of others, in our prayers. We must remember that Jesus urged us to make our needs known to the Father, and He linked our faith, our needs, and our prayer. Often we wonder if intercessory prayer will be answered, as the years go by without an answer. Yet one day our prayer's answer comes back on golden wings and we know how Augustine's mother must have felt when, after twenty years, her prayers for her son's conversion were answered.

Keeping a list of those persons and concerns for whom we are praying is a good idea. Only in such a way will we really notice when many of our prayers are fulfilled. Not all of our requests will be answered as we desire, as even Paul discovered in his prayers for healing (2 Cor. 12:8-9). When we make our petitions to God, we must do so in sincerity and honesty, with an openness to accept whatever God's will may be and with a trust and confidence in God. George Muller is a beautiful example of a Spirit-led man whose life demonstrates the power of intercessory prayer.

Scripture

I mention this element at this point because in my own experience, after quietness, meditation, and prayer, I am ready to turn to the Bible either in a devotional fashion or for deeper study. The Bible is helpful in the earlier meditation time as an aid in developing an attitude of prayer. But having already done that, I can seek spiritual growth and guidance through the Word.

Some plan for reading and studying the Bible is necessary, and there are many good approaches. You can start at Genesis and proceed book by book or maybe select a favorite book or one which has perhaps been neglected. Perhaps a theme or word study is what you choose. Once the plan is decided, you move to deal with a daily portion, determined by natural divisions in the text. Using imagination to put yourself in the Scripture scene may be helpful. With which character do you identify, and why? What are the colors, the smells, the sounds of the passage? If you were the person or part of the group in the center of the passage, what would your response be? What should it be? What examples are in the passage for you?

When a passage strikes a new chord in our hearts, we can pause and offer that truth to God in prayer and thank Him for it. Some passages are appropriate to dwell upon and turn around and offer as prayers, especially sections of Paul's letters. We must constantly let the Scripture speak to us, by the quickening power of the Spirit. Think on the Word, imagine about the Word, apply the Word, resolve to walk in the light of the Word. And we must add the encouragement of memorizing those Scripture verses which especially speak to us during the devotional time.

Journal

Many Christians through the centuries have found the keeping of spiritual journals or diaries to be great spiritual help. In fact, many of the spiritual classics started out as accounts of God's working in individual hearts, such as *Confessions* by Augustine, *Journal of John Woolman, Life and Diary of David Brainerd,* and *Journal of John Wesley.* We are inclined to protest that we have no intention of being in that class, but neither did they! Nevertheless, while journal keeping is not for everybody, for several reasons make it an idea worth trying for a while.

Most importantly, keeping journals help us remember that we are on pilgrimage. And, from time to time, we should examine our journals to check our spiritual progress. Whatever we write is worth recording. Our journals can become the vantage points from which we can see the waves of our spiritual sea toss and roll.

What sorts of things shall we put in our journals? A good first entry is a candid spiritual assessment—briefly written. Goals for our lives in the Spirit are fitting, as well as daily reflections of our spiritual growth. Our gleanings from Scripture and ideas for further study could be a part of our entry. In difficult times, we can record our honest feelings and prayers; later we will be grateful to see how God rescues His children. Those persons and concerns for whom we pray ought to be part of our record too. Remember: Be honest, be brief, and be sure to date each entry. One other suggestion—try writing a prayer every now and then in the journal.

The Holy Spirit's Part in Prayer

So often we do not know how to pray or for what we should pray or even have the inner desire to pray. In these areas, the Holy Spirit plays a vital part in our devotional lives. Several key Scriptures relate the Spirit to prayer.

"Likewise the Spirit also helpeth our infirmities: for we know not what we should pray for as we ought: but the Spirit itself maketh intercession for us with groanings which cannot be uttered" (Rom. 8:26). We are clearly told that there are times when we ought to pray but do not know what to say or how to say it. But we are not to worry; the Spirit will speak for us. Galatians 4:6 tells us that, because we are the children of God, the Holy Spirit within us teaches and urges us to call upon our Heavenly Father as a father.

Ephesians 6:18 speaks of our prayers always being "in the Spirit," while Jude 20 urges us to build up our faith through prayer "in the Holy [Spirit]" James 5:16 says, "The effectual fervent prayer of a righteous man availeth much." More literally, and clearly, it says that the prayer being "wrought in us," that is, by the Holy Spirit, has great power.

While there is a definite relationship between the Holy Spirit and praying in "unknown tongues," that is certainly not the primary expression of the Spirit's work in prayer. What can we say about this area of His work?

Effective Prayer Depends Upon the Spirit

At least five areas of our prayer lives depend upon the Spirit for life and depth. First, the indwelling Spirit quietens our hearts in devotion, stands between us and the disruptive work of Satan, and turns our minds and hearts toward God. Second, the Spirit blesses our diligence in meditation and study of the Scripture and efforts at prayer. We are strengthened by the Spirit's encouragement.

Third, the Spirit inclines us to pray. Have we closed our eyes and lifted our hearts in prayer and experienced a wonderful desire just to adore and praise and thank God? That is surely the Spirit's work. Fourth, He often gives us liberty in prayer. That is, when our hearts are burdened, and perhaps the subject of our prayer is heavy, the Spirit allows our feelings to flow easily into words, laying before the Father's throne the depth of our desire and concern.

Fifth, the Spirit actually prays for us. In those times of deep concern, deep disappointment, deep hope too heavy, too real, and pressing to put into words—when we can only cry in anguish, "O my Father!"—we know our kindest and most understanding Friend, the Holy Spirit, is pleading our case before the throne of God. C. H. Dodd's comment that, in the Spirit's interceding when we cannot pray, we see "the divine in us appealing to the God above us" is both enlightening and profound.[17] And sixth, the Spirit illuminates our prayers and motivates us to action. Prayer is more than our speaking to God; it is our waiting upon God for guidance and instruction. The Spirit plants the certainty of particular courses of action in our hearts while we are yet on our knees. The Spirit floods our hearts with assurance and forgiveness and love as we pour out our hearts in prayer.

Yet we must be careful. We need to remember that our prayers are to be in the will and spirit of Jesus. Only then can we expect the Spirit's help. To deceive either ourselves or others by claiming the guidance of the Spirit upon selfish prayers or selfish actions derived from prayer is sin. The corrective for this danger is to pray for the power and presence of the Spirit to be felt in our hearts as we pray.

The Spirit, Our Helper

When I was barely a teenager, I began working in the shade tobacco farms in our county, as did many of my friends. I well remember the first day I worked. My job was to help unload the sleds on which were great stretchers loaded with tobaccos leaves. A huge man had the other end, and he never got tired! Toward the end of the afternoon, I began to see I would not survive the day; I could hardly reach out far enough on either side to grasp the big stretcher handles, my back and arms were about to break, and my hands weren't big enough to grip the handles firmly. We only had to carry the stretcher some fifty feet or so, but with each step my grip loosened. On one stretcher, late in the afternoon, I just ran out of steam. As my hands began to slip on the handles, I knew I couldn't make it; I would have to drop the sled in front of all the workers—a terrible embarrassment for a boy of thirteen. I grasped the handles harder and harder, squinched my eyes—and then a big hand closed over mine as a man standing near saw my plight and stepped up behind me to help. Through the years that incident has always been a picture to me of how the Holy Spirit helps us, even in our prayer lives. He is there in time of need to help.

Pray Without Ceasing

The four living creatures in the Book of Revelation never cease saying, "Holy, holy, holy, Lord God Almighty, which was, and is, and is to come" (4:8). Is it possible that the Scriptures really teach that *we* should "Pray without ceasing," as read in 1 Thessalonians 5:17?

Defining Unceasing Prayer

Considering unceasing prayer moves us from the stated daily devotional time to a daily twenty-four-hour prayer vigil! Tradition says that James, the brother of Jesus and leader of the Jerusalem church, had callouses on his knees from praying. Perhaps he could be a model for such unceasing prayer as the Bible seems to command.

Yet when we think about it, to pray without ceasing is really not difficult; we do it already. Isn't it true that prayer is really more than a posture or the addressing of words to a god—that prayer is rather the pointing of our lives and wills and energies toward some ruling desire or dream? If we want more than anything else in the world to be Queen of May, or to be rich, or to be like a movie star, are not these our gods and are not all our efforts turned to them? Are we not in a constant state of prayer to these gods? The need of Christians is to focus our hearts' desire upon God and desire His fellowship most of all. Then to Him we shall pray without ceasing.

The immature, carnal Christian lives on the level of activities. For that person spirituality may be merely attending church with some regularity and perhaps having a blessing before the meal. As the Christian becomes serious about his prayer life and establishes a regular devotional time, he may wobble back and forth between the activity-oriented spiritual life and the growing interior life. As he becomes a mature Christian, he will both have a regular prayer time and an awareness of God throughout the day.

This development of continual practice of the presence of God needs to become a part of our characters. We need to become aware of this great salvation we possess, this great Teacher within—the Holy Spirit. We must become aware of both our spiritual needs and spiritual resources so that, throughout the day, "deep calls unto deep," need is lifted to the abundance, and loneliness is lifted to fellowship. Whatever the physical posture, the soul can be on its knees.

Cultivating Unceasing Prayer

How can we cultivate unceasing prayer which is a characteristic of devotional maturity. First, we can develop the stated devotional time—that regular, eagerly awaited time of communion when other concerns are laid aside and we rest our arms awhile on the windowsill of heaven. That daily time will become the reservoir from which we will drink of the living water throughout the day.

Second, we can think positively about developing a sense of God's presence. We can refuse to let our changing moods dictate either our stated devotional time or the cultivation of God's presence. We can imagine Jesus sitting beside our desks or riding beside us in our cars. For example, I remember vividly that one day while driving, in the midst of audible prayer, I turned to direct the prayer to Jesus beside me in the car. It was an unconscious act, yet it showed me how real my prayers ought always to be.

Throughout the day, we are confronted by many hindrances to the development of this attitude of the presence of God. Our guilt for past sins will poison such spiritual work, if we allow. Our present sin, that is, those things we may do during the day that we know are displeasing to God, will dry up and choke off our conscious effort to be mindful of His presence, if we allow. Our worldliness, our busyness, our uncomfortable feelings of "being more religious"—or our prideful feeling of such—are all possible saboteurs to our lives of unceasing prayer.

The key to keeping the daily appointment to "fill the reservoir" and to clean up our lives as we move through our days is spiritual discipline. We can know we are making progress when, in moments of recovery from a lapse of awareness of the Spirit, we realize we had not really completely

forgotten Him. Such flashes of realization help us remember Him who
dwells within us.

The Results of the Devotional Life

Our world today is morally bankrupt. People live their lives with no
meaningful relationship to God and no understanding of the value and
nature of His moral laws. When we try to share the glory of the life in
Christ with such people, one of their first reactions is that they do not see
that God and His holy will have made *our* lives any more meaningful.
One of the things deeper devotional lives will do for us is present more
integrated, fulfilled life-styles before the world. And the world desper-
ately needs to see that.

Another result of deeper devotional lives is that we will become reservoirs, not mere canals. Many of us in leadership positions in churches
and religious groups have heavy spiritual demands upon us, but we are
too shallow, so much like a canal that we have no spiritual abundance or
depth. We need to develop spiritual reservoirs in our lives, out of which
we may draw the living water as needed to minister.

A true devotional life is a paradox. On the one hand it tears one loose
from worldly attachments and ambitions. Yet is also brings alive a divine, if painful, concern for the world. As Kelly put it, "He plucks the
world out of our hearts, lossening the chains of attachment. And He
hurls the world into our hearts, where we and He together carry it in
infinitely tender love."[18]

The devotional life is like learning to ride a bicycle. As we learn, we
wobble and sometimes fall. But if we keep at it, the joy and satisfaction is
like that time when you finally ride the bike for fifty years on your own.
Sheer joy!

Notes

1. Evelyn Underhill, *Concerning the Inner Life with the House of the Soul*
(New York: E.P. Dutton and Co., Inc. [n.d.]), p. 22.

2. Thomas R. Kelly, *A Testament of Devotion*, p. 119.

3. Fanny Crosby, "I Am Thine, O Lord."

4. Evelyn Underhill, *Mystics of the Church*, p. 10.

5. Wayne E. Oates, *The Psychology of Religion* (Waco: Word Books, 1973), pp. 118-119.

6. Bernard of Clairvaux

7. Bruce Bernard, *The Bible and Its Painters* (New York: MacMillan, 1983).

8. Samuel Miller, *The Life of the Soul* (Waco: Word Books, 1951), p. 126.

9. A. H. McNeile, *Devotion and Discipleship* (London: W. Heffer and Sons Ltd., 1934), p. 15.

10. Douglas V. Steere, in foreward to Thomas Merton, *Contemplative Prayer* (London: Daton, Longman, and Todd, 1973), p. 8.

11. Terry C. Muck, "10 Questions About the Devotional Life," *Leadership* (Spring 1982), p. 32.

12. Underhill, *Concerning the Inner Life*, pp. 65-66.

13. Leslie D. Weatherhead, *A Private House of Prayer* (Nashville: Abingdon, 1958), pp. 5-19.

14. Buttrick, *Prayer* (Nashville: Abingdon Press, 1942), pp. 257-58.

15. Alexander Whyte, *Lancelot Andrewes and His Private Devotions* (London: Oliphant Anderson and Ferrier, 1896), p. 12.

16. Ibid., pp. 170-173.

17. C. H. Dodd, *The Epistle of Paul to the Romans*, p. 150.

18. Kelly, p. 47.

6

The Development
Do I Have Spiritual Gifts
and Spiritual Fruit?

In our study of the life in the Spirit, we have explored many of the concepts and images of what our spiritual lives ought to be. We have looked at such contrasting ways of life as the old man and the new, the flesh and the spirit, and the realities of sonship and the crucifixion of our old selves. We have thought about the dynamics which shape our spiritual lives and realized that the Holy Spirit needs to be given a more prominent role in our thinking and teaching and living. We have spent time reflecting on the crucial importance of our devotional life, for it is the soil in which the Spirit works.

Now we will explore the visible results in the individual Christian's life of this state of sonship, this walking in the Spirit, this mature devotional life. Only such a life is in tune with God, available and pliable and ready to be used. Two primary areas will occupy our attention in this chapter: the gifts of the Spirit and the fruit of the Spirit. We will also discuss how we can discover and use our spiritual gifts, as well as the danger of grieving and quenching the Spirit, and committing the unpardonable sin.

We generally turn to the lists of spiritual gifts found in Paul's writings to describe the gifted Christian, but many of these gifts are to be seen in the lives of Stephen and Barnabas. Stephen first comes to our attention as one in whom the church saw the ability and concern to care for the needs of the poor, a *helper* and *administrator*. Stephen is famous for his *preaching*—in clear, intelligible speech. Barnabas is an example of one who freely and lovingly gave to the church. He was also an *encourager* as he endorsed Paul before the church. Along with Paul he became an *evangelist* to the Gentiles. Stephen and Barnabas were *charismatic*, that is, gifted Christians. The word *charismatic* simply means gifted and comes from the Greek word *charis,* often translated "grace."

Misconceptions About Spiritual Gifts

For many people, the phrase *charismatic Christians* brings to mind either a smiling, outgoing, baby-kissing, politician-type personality or a shouting, emotional, tongue-speaking Christian. The biblical idea of charisma is neither of these. Modern secular ideas of charisma need to be separated from the New Testament idea, seen most clearly in Paul's first letter to the Corinthians.

Always a Sensational Gift?

The first misconception is that spiritual gifts are always sensational, dealing with the miraculous or exceptional. Coupled with this is the idea that the possessor of such gifts must be highly emotional and, when under the influence of the Spirit, out of personal control. This perception is simply not true. Some spiritual gifts, such as speaking in tongues and healings, were and are rather sensational; but these are not the primary gifts and ought not characterize the whole. These spectacular gifts did not play a dominant role in the early church; in fact, we would never have heard about tongues were it not for the misuse of this gift in Corinth. Notice in 1 Corinthians 14 that Paul did not, however, reject these gifts, but sought only to control them. Those gifts most highly praised by Paul are the more helpful but less sensational, such as prophecy, teaching, and love.

For a Favored Few?

The second misconception is that spiritual gifts are only for a favored few. Sometimes we tend to think of spiritual gifts as being only for those involved in professional ministry—preachers and church staff members, evangelists, and missionaries, and seminary teachers. How sad and wrong is such as idea! Spiritual gifts are for all God's children—*every Christian is charismatic!* Every Christian has received the baptism of the Spirit: every Christian has been set apart and sanctified; and every Christian has been given some spiritual gift, according to Scripture (1 Cor. 12:7). While no one person receives *all* the spiritual gifts, by the same token, no Christian is without a spiritual gift. Each person is given *one or more* gifts. "To each his own" is a fundamental principle of the biblically charismatic church. Spiritual gifts are expressions and channels of Christians' calling in Christ. Nobody goes away empty-handed, and every church member's gift is essential if the church is to glorify Christ. No one should seek a particular gift, unless it be the gift of love, as Paul so beautifully expressed in 1 Corinthians 13 and its context.

A Sign of Maturity and Authority?

The third misconception is that certain spiritual gifts carry with them authority and a guarantee of spiritual maturity. This misconception seems often to be tied to the more ecstatic gifts, such as tongues. The very realization that *every* Christian receives a spiritual gift or gifts at conversion ought to help us realize there is no necessary relationship between gift and spiritual maturity. Hopefully, the realization and responsibility of the gifts would lead to maturity in all cases, and it seems essential in the case of Christians with the gifts of preaching and teaching the faith.

My experience has been that spiritual maturity and tongues, for instance, do not necessarily go hand in hand. I well remember a young lady who felt she had the gift of tongues and also felt that if God wanted her to stop smoking He would tell her! Often a kind of spiritual superiority, or pecking order, develops with the realization of gifts in a church. This is scripturally wrong. Just as all Christians are gifted, so all Christians are still sinful human beings. One of the worst mistakes we can make is to assume that those with more visible gifts are more like Christ. We not only deceive ourselves but also lead such gifted persons to let down their guard against Satan. We witness, from time to time, the tragic falls of gifted ministers who began to believe they were above temptation or more spiritual than others simply because of the possession of particular spiritual gifts. Every Christian and his gift is essential; none can be overlooked and each has a proper authority, but we must not try to deduce claims and privileges or spiritual maturity from our gifts.

Gifts or Talents?

The fourth misconception is that our natural endowments, or talents, are the same as our spiritual gifts. Not so—the unbeliever may have a natural ability to play the piano and may play for the devil in a honky-tonk. We may use our natural talents for the Lord, and our gifts may use and heighten the natural ability; but the spiritual gifts are given at our conversion by the Holy Spirit for the edifying of the church.

The Charismatic Church

Gifts Build the Church

The only valid outcome of the spiritual gifts is the strengthening of the local church. While the Holy Spirit manifests Himself in the lives of individual Christians, this diversity and portioning out of gifts has the unity and functioning of the entire church as its goal. *With* one another *for* one another is the biblical use of gifts. Hopefully our spiritual gifts will lead to our individual Christian growth and edification, but their stated bibilical purpose is the building up of the church.

Nowhere in 1 Corinthians 12—14, the keynote passage on the purpose of the spiritual gifts, is the emphasis on the individual's gain. Rather, the emphasis is on the building up, equipping, and ministry of the church as a whole. First Corinthians 12 and Ephesians 4 stress this unity in difference with the building up of the total church as the goal. Paul asked if all parts of the body are hands or ears or eyes? All are different, yet needed. We may pay little attention to our toes until we bang them on the bedpost—but then we know they exist! A broken arm teaches us how much we need that arm. Some people no longer have the use of an eye or ear, an arm or leg, and they do get along; but God's intention is for the full use of our complete bodies. Our churches will be transformed when we grasp that truth and apply it to our churches, which frequently limp along because we neglect our spiritual gifts.

Guidelines for Gifts

Before we examine the individual gifts mentioned in Scripture, let us note that along with this structure of gifts there needs to be some guidelines to keep unity and order. Otherwise the more emotional gifts can be destructive, as in Corinth.

Three guidelines for the use of spiritual gifts were developed by Paul. First, nobody speaking under the guidance of the Spirit can curse Jesus (1 Cor. 12:3). Second, the gift is of God only if it builds up the church. And, third, the gifts must be used in a spirit of love to avoid creating confusion in the church. The church itself is to use these guidelines to judge the utterances and actions of its members in the use of supposed spiritual gifts. And there is at least some ranking of the gifts in value, since in 1 Corinthians 14 prophecy is valued above tongues.

Another controlling and unifying factor in the use of spiritual gifts is Paul's insistence that we, as gifted Christians, are still in control of our minds and bodies even when exercising our gifts. "And the spirits of the prophets are subject to the prophets"(1 Cor. 14:32). The ecstatic speaker perhaps cannot decide *what* he will say, but he can decide *whether* to say it and *when* to stop.

Some may think it strange for Paul—and us—to deal at length with guidelines and safeguards in the use of spiritual gifts, but the first Christians soon saw that spiritual gifts can be abused. Even the right use of gifts can spring from mixed motives, and the gifts can hold hands with ignorance, weakness, and error. The reality of spiritual gifts—the amazing and powerful truth that every Christian is charismatic—is an untapped spiritual storehouse in most churches.

The Gifts Bestowed

The Lists of the Gifts

There are four biblical lists of spiritual gifts, and others are scattered throughout the New Testament, such as celibacy (1 Cor. 7:7). The four lists are found in Romans 12:6-8; 1 Corinthians 12:8-10; 1 Corinthians 12:28-30; and Ephesians 4:11. A total of thirty gifts appear on the various lists; but many are duplicated, leaving only nineteen actual gifts mentioned.

The lists are quite different, with no apparent attempt to mention exactly the same gifts. These lists seem to be only representative, and perhaps Paul simply put down those gifts which came to mind when writing or those of which he had knowledge in those churches. The lists can hardly be taken together as an official list of gifts with no other possibilities, since, as pointed out above, Paul failed to list one of his own gifts, celibacy.

The order in which the gifts appear on the different lists varies, although a particular gift will appear in each list in the same general area such as the top, middle, or bottom of the group. In this there does seem to be some effort at ranking the gifts in value. For instance, prophecy or prophets rank either first or second in all four lists, while tongues and their interpretation appear in only two lists and both times are at the bottom.

The Nature of the Gifts

In some of the lists the gifts are seen as endowments or abilities, such as prophecy, while the same manifestation is expressed in another list as a *person with that ability,* or grace gift, such as a prophet. I think there is no significance in that difference. In 1 Corinthians 12:4-6 Paul, in his preface to listing spiritual gifts, referred to them as gifts, administrations, and operations. I am comfortable with organizing these lists in five different kinds of gifts, those dealing with speech, mind, material realm, church organization, and the spread of the gospel. Such divisions are simply for convenience. The stated gifts are only representative of perhaps many more unmentioned.

The gifts of speech include prophecy, teaching, exhorting, tongues, and the interpretation of tongues. Gifts associated with the mind are wisdom and knowledge. Gifts related to the material realm include ministry, giving, mercy, faith, healing, and miracles. Gifts for church organization are ruling, discerning of spirits, helps, and pastors. Gifts for the spread of the gospel include apostles and evangelists.

Prophecy (Prophets)

The gift of prophecy is one of intelligible speech which illuminates God's will for all humanity or for a given situation in the church. It certainly includes preaching the good news of Jesus for the conviction of conscience. Prophets speak out for God, out of the deep things of God. It seems to be the most highly valued gift (1 Cor. 14:39). Examples of persons possessing this gift include Peter (Acts 2:14-36) and Judas and Silas (Acts 15:32). Some ecstatic utterances could have been included in this gift, since Paul reminded the Corinthian church that the prophets *can* keep their spirits under control (1 Cor. 14:32).

Teaching

Persons with this gift were linked with pastors in Ephesians 4:11 and were probably folk who worked with settled congregations, handing on and teaching the faith to new Christians. The teacher sheds light on doctrine and systematizes the faith for the church. He has an important ministry with new Christians.

Exhortation

The word is *paraclete:* "to call along side of." One who has this gift is an encourager to those who need words of affirmation or hope. This gift may belong to the prophet or the giver of the administrator. Barnabas, in his relationship to Paul and John Mark, is a good example. While this exhorting may be a private, one-on-one ministry, it may also be used in a similar fashion as preaching.

Tongues and Interpretation of Tongues

The gifts of tongues and the interpretation of tongues was not nearly so prominent in the early church as we might think or as some may say who so highly value this gift. "Speaking in tongues" has to do with an ecstatic utterance, maybe in prayer, in which the conscious mind does not exercise control as it does in normal speech. This speech must be translated into an understandable message for the church to have any spiritual gain from its use. In Scripture these gifts seem to be the most elementary of the gifts, or expressions of the Spirit, in the believer's life. Today they are subject to much misuse and were a source of grief at Corinth.

Nevertheless, they are valid gifts, and the ambiguous biblical attitude toward them is heightened by the fact that Paul said he possessed the gift of speaking in tongues! Practically every sympathic passage about tongues is qualified with a warning or restraint (1 Cor. 14:4-5,18,39). Paul commanded the women to refrain completely from tongues in the church service (compare 1 Cor. 11:3-10 with 14:34-35; the latter is a reference to tongues). The strongest word of warning and assessment is given when Paul said that he valued five words in intelligible speech to ten thousand words in an unknown tongue (1 Cor. 14:19).

Wisdom and Knowledge

These two gifts are associated with our minds. The gift of wisdom seems to be the ability to speak with exceptional wisdom in especially difficult situations. It "enables one to discern in the dramas of history the counsel of God."[1] By wisdom we know the true value of things, for it is spiritual insight and comprehension.

Distinguishing between the gift of wisdom and the gift of knowledge is not easy. Wisdom seems to be the broader term, with knowledge being the intellectual grasp of the truths of the gospel. Perhaps the gift of knowledge is related as well to the ability to refer to facts not known by natural means, as when a preacher makes a reference to some matter in a sermon and it seems to some hearer that he knows his or her heart.

Ministry, Giving, and Mercy

The gifts of ministry, giving, and mercy are to be used in the material realm and are clear in their meaning. Some Christians simply have as a gift from the Holy Spirit the temperament, ability, and desire to minister to the needs of the shut-in, the poor, and many others. Some Christians have no gift for teaching, for instance, but receive a deep joy in giving of their wealth and seem to have insight into where the need is. Others are, by their grace gift, persons of exceptional mercy and tenderness. They possess a treasure of empathy in the presence of human misery.

Faith

The gift of faith is not so easily understood. Obviously this is not saving faith, for all Christians already possess that. This gift seems to be the ability to trust God for things to happen that are beyond the normal experience as when, for instance, Jeremiah bought a field just before Judah was taken into the Exile because he had faith in God's power. This gift is a kind of openness and confidence that enables the power of God to operate through a person who has it. It also seems to produce both miracles and martyrs.

Healing

The gift of healing is another gift which is open to much interpretation. Views of the meaning of this gift range from seeing it as exercised by Christian physicians to seeing validation for anointing, prayer cloths, and the like to the view that this gift is a "sign gift" which was given to the first generation of Christians and those today who first carry the gospel to new cultures as an authenticating sign. Under this last view, the gift of healing has disappeared from Christian culture.

Many of us will not be sure how this gift is exercised or just who may have it, but we will remember that faith healers who operate apart from the building up of the church, who work in a sensational and self-praising manner which cannot be verified, do not meet the general guidelines for the spiritual gifts of the New Testament.

Words from three scholars state our feelings rather well. Dale Moody says, "quackery that excludes modern medicine, on the part of misguided advocates, and panic, on the part of those who are skeptical, have all but eliminated this ministry so normal in the apostolic era."[2] The middle approach between quackery and skepticism is voiced by W. A. Criswell and Frank Stagg, respectively: "If there are gifts of divine healing they ought to be employed in a hospital, up and down the corridors; not in a tent, up and down the aisles."[3] And, "if there are those today who have special access to divine power to heal, they then have tremendous responsibility. There are many who are blind, deaf, lame, or suffering the almost unbearable pain of cancer. If some have the power, others of us have the list. Let's get the two together."[4] In the end, the question is certainly not one of what God *can* do but what He *does* and in what manner.

Miracles

The gift of miracles seem to be best understood as mighty works apart from healing, such as the blinding of Elymas by Paul (Acts 13:8-11). This gift, like that of healing and tongues, are seen by some as "sign" gifts which disappeared after Christianity became established. A study of Hebrews 2:3-4 does, indeed, say that our great salvation was attested by miracles and signs and wonders to the *first* generation, but not to the second generation, to which the writer belonged. Some folk feel these signs will return in the last days. However this may be, we will keep in mind that God can work mighty wonders whenever He chooses.

Gifts for the Organized Church

Four gifts seem best seen in relationship to the work of the organized church: ruling (administration), the discernment of spirits, helps, and pastors. The discerning of spirits has to do with discovering the source of ecstatic utterances and keeping control and unity and order in the church. Administration has always been needed in the church from the days of the complaints of the widows in Acts 6:1. The Greek word can be translated "helpful deeds." This gift has to do with assisting the church leaders in ministry and may equally apply to the help given the elderly and needy. Pastors are shepherds who guide, feed, protect, and nurture the flock entrusted to them—God's church.

Apostles and Evangelists

The spread of the gospel is related to the gifts of apostles and evangelists. As in some other cases, the gifts are bound up in persons so closely as to speak of the actual persons as the gift. Obviously the apostles are more than the historical twelve and possibly refer to the gift of those who establish new churches and begin new fields of work. The evangelists are those who have the ability to proclaim the basic facts of saving grace to the lost; they differ from pastors in that pastors appear to have a more settled ministry which edifies those already saved.

The Giver of the Gifts

A proper understanding of spiritual gifts begins and ends with the Giver of those gifts. All the spiritual gifts are expressions of God's grace and power and are put into the lives of God's people to point toward the one great gift of salvation in Christ. Paul spoke of the gifts as given by the Spirit (1 Cor. 12:28), by Christ (Eph. 4:11), and by God (1 Cor. 12:6). Clearly Paul made no distinction in the Godhead here. The Lord who places in each Christian's life at least one spiritual gift also places within that life the power and ability to use that gift. Likewise the church has been given every gift needed to carry out its work if all its members will seek, find, and use their gifts.

Discovering Our Spiritual Gift

How can we discover our particular spiritual gifts and use them as the gifted Christians we are? Several steps may help us find our gifts.

We Find Through Seeking

First, we must have a desire, a yearning to fill this gap in our Christian experience. This desire will be born of our realization that the Bible teaches the importance of our using our spiritual gifts, and we may need to begin by making a careful and in-depth study of the gifts. The desire may develop from a realization of the needs of our own churches. As we study the Bible, in what areas are our churches weak? If every member were walking in the Spirit, including the use of their spiritual gifts, there would be no weaknesses. Our awareness may include, along with the doctrine of gifts and the state of our churches, an evaluation of our own ministries through our churches. What are we doing for God through our churches?

We Receive Through Asking

Second, we must be open to whatever gifts God may have for us. Our sense of expectation should lead us to the third step, that of asking God for guidance and revelation concerning our gifts. Luke 11:5-13 records the parable of the unwilling person who nevertheless gave bread to a friend. The point is a contrast: God is not like that! "And I say unto you, Ask, and it shall be given you; seek, and ye shall find; knock, and it shall be opened unto you. If ye then, being evil, know how to give good gifts unto your children: how much more shall your heavenly Father give the Holy Spirit to them that ask Him?" (vv. 9, 13). The asking must be from the proper motive of being used to build up Christ's church and in the realization of our own lack of power.

We Experiment to Discover

With a confidence that God knows us best, and having placed our openness before Him, a fourth step is to ask questions of our own personalities and experiences. Where has God already used us in the past? Do any of the gifts earlier in this chapter seem like us? What do we enjoy doing? What gifts do our churches seem to need? A church which always needs more teachers, for instance, is either misorganized and needs someone with the gift of administration or needs more of its members to discover their gift of teaching.

The sixth step is to experiment. We can talk to our pastors and share our search with them. If we think certain gifts are ours, we can ask the pastor to help us find ways to put those gifts in service to the church for six months or so. This should help us confirm that we have those gifts or we will realize we should continue searching. And seventh, we should rejoice in the discovery of our gifts. Gifts are to be celebrated.

The Fruit of the Spirit

If we truly desire to be led of the Holy Spirit, if we develop rich and mature devotional lives, if we seek and find our spiritual gifts, we will bear the beautiful ethical fruit of the Spirit. In Matthew 7 Jesus spoke of how a person would be known by his fruit (vv. 15-23). In John 15 Jesus said those who abide in Him bear much fruit and in that bearing of fruit is the Father glorified (vv. 1-8).

Paul spelled out the meaning and definition of spiritual fruit. He tied its presence to our conscious cooperation with the Holy Spirit: "If we live in the Spirit, let us also walk in the Spirit" (Gal. 5:25). The fruit of the Spirit is more than mere life or label. A paper label can tell the species of a tree, and the leaves can proclaim life; the fruit is more than label or leaf—it is the purpose for which the tree exists.[5] To have fruit we must be rooted in the Spirit. As naturally as apples grow on apple trees, spiritual fruit will be produced in the lives of those led by the Spirit.

Spiritual Gifts and Fruit of the Spirit

Spiritual gifts are given to each Christian for power, for service, for ministry to the upbuilding of the church. The gifts have to do with our outer life of service. Inner spiritual qualities are the fruit of the Spirit. The gifts are for action, the graces of the fruit of the Spirit are for ethics, a shaping of the character of Christians—the inner life. The various spiritual gifts are distributed throughout the congregation; one here, two in that life, and so forth. A single spiritual gift may find perfect expression in our lives, and we will not feel slighted or lacking because we have only one; but all nine graces of the fruit of the Spirit should be seen in *every* Christian. All the graces are needed for our characters to be pleasing to God.

The Nine Graces in Three Groups

The relationship to God.—Galatians 5:22-23 lists the fruit of the Spirit: love, joy, peace, longsuffering, gentleness, goodness, faith, meekness, temperance. These graces seem to naturally fall into three groups of three relationships. The relationship to God is expressed in the love, joy, and peace of God. Without these, Christians cannot be expected to bear spiritual fruit. The power and motivation to act ethically are provided as we possess these graces of God. On the basis of this relationship to God, we can then relate rightly to others.

The relationship to others.—The second triad of graces—longsuffering, gentleness, goodness—deals with our relationships to other persons. These are the qualities needed to relate to other people in a Christlike manner. Indeed, all nine graces find their perfect fulfillment in Jesus.

The relationship to our inner selves.—The third group—faith, meekness, and temperance—refer to our inner selves. These last three graces were famous Hellenic ethical qualities highly prized in the biblical times. Paul, in listing them last, may have wanted to suggest that the fruit of the Spirit transforms and goes beyond both the demands of the Jewish law and the Greek ideals. We must realize that, as with Spiritual gifts, so with the fruit of the Spirit, we must put all our human will and strength at the Spirit's disposal. From the human side of our spiritual experience, we are called to "hallow" ourselves, to refuse to conform to this world.

Love

The love which is to grace our character is *agapē* love—God's kind of love, a care and concern for others which does not count the cost and is based on the sacredness of each person in God's sight. It is not a love based on self-interest, such as sexual love *(eros)* or brotherly love *(philo)*. *Agapē* love is, of course, beautifully and best described in 1 Corinthians 13, where it is seen in the context of gifts. Queen of the Christian graces, this kind of love never fails or fades; when it is genuine in our lives it is, as Henry Drummond said, the greatest thing in the world.

Joy

The joy which is a fruit of the Spirit is far different from the world's concept of pleasure or even mirth or humor. A person can be a world-renowned humorist and spend a life making others laugh, and yet be cynical and bitter. Mark Twain, for instance, summed up his view of life in these tragic words:

> The burden of pain, care, misery, grows heavier year by year; at length ambition is dead; pride is dead; vanity is dead; longing for release is in their place. It comes at last—the only unpoisoned gift earth ever had for them—and they vanish from a world where they were of no consequence, where they achieved nothing, where they were a mistake and a failure and a foolishness: where they left no sign that they ever existed—a world which will lament them a day and forget them forever.[6]

Contrary to such a view is Christian joy, of which Paul wrote to the Philippian church. This kind of joy runs deep and can even link hands with sorrow and affliction (1 Thess. 1:6), for it is a deep sense of fulfillment through our relationship to Christ which lets us celebrate our lives even in the midst of changing scenes.

Peace

Peace that passes understanding (Phil. 4:7) and is the foundation for joy is a fruit of the Spirit. This peace is impossible until we lay down our arms of rebellion against God. It is a tranquillity of mind based on the assurance of a right relationship to God. Until we are forgiven of God, forgive others, and learn to forgive ourselves, we will not make the kind of progress toward this fruit that God intends.

Long-suffering

Long-suffering literally means "long-tempered." That is the opposite of short-tempered and, in the Bible, is often listed as a feature of God's character (Eph. 4:2; Col. 3:13; Mark 9:19). It is the power to put up with the problems, frustrations, and ill-treatments of life. An incident in the life of George Washington Carver shows how this grace can shine in a person's character. This great black Christian educator and scientist once got off a train in a Southern city en route to a speaking engagement. The white cab driver eagerly searched for his important passenger, but when he realized the passenger was black, he refused to drive him! Dr. Carver studied the situation a moment and then announced, "All right, you get in back and I'll drive *you*!" And with that he climbed up on the driver's box and took the reins. Dr. Carver's motto was, "I will allow no man to make me hate him!" This is the fruit of the Spirit known as long-suffering. It is the power to stand up under the load of life.

Gentleness

Gentleness, sometimes translated *kindness*, has as its root the idea of usefulness. Gentleness is not seen as useful in the world's eyes. Yet genuine conversion always leads to a display of a kindlier spirit toward others. As Wordsworth said,

> His heart is opening more and more,
> A holy sense pervades his mind;

> He feels what he for human kind
> Had never felt before.[7]

Goodness

This is more than righteousness. We all know of righteous folk who are stern and unloving. The Puritans have certainly been labeled as stern, cold, and righteous, whether true or not. A good man, in the sense of this fruit of the Spirit, has all the moral virtues of the righteous man, plus a kindliness and warmth to others. Romans 5:7 refers to the positive reaction others have to a person who has developed this virtue.

Faith

Faith is the only fruit of the Spirit actually listed as a spiritual gift by Paul (1 Cor. 12:9). As a fruit of the Spirit, faith is not a power, but a grace-adorning character. It is the grace of resting in God, free from anxiety. All of us can think of Christian friends whose lives bear this fruit of the Spirit, a resting, abiding faith whate'er betide. *Reliability* may better express this grace. That is, the Christian whose character is adorned by faith is a person who can be relied upon. The Quakers have historically been good examples of such a faith character. Their reliability and trustworthiness was acknowledged even by those who persecuted them! When put in prison, they were often left unguarded because their simple word not to escape was sufficient. Sometimes they were transferred from prison to prison without escort, for the same reason!

Meekness

A genuine consideration for others and a willingness to turn loose of our rights if that will benefit another are elements to the virtue of meekness. We need to clear our minds of the thought that meekness is weakness. Meekness is strength under control. This virtue is often seen in Paul, and springs from a deep dependence on God and a quiet acceptance of whatever God's will may bring.

Self-control

Some people's lives are controlled by the advertising of the media; some people's lives are controlled by instincts and animal drives and greed. The grace of self-control is developed in the life of the Christian as one lives under the lordship of Jesus. He knows no man can serve two masters; he who keeps his own body under control lest, as Paul said, "he become a castaway." *Temperance* is a worn translation for this virtue since that word has become tied to the misuse of alcohol. The idea of self-control is much broader, and in our time needs to take on fresh meaning as we especially resist the control of mass media.

The bearing of the fruit of the Spirit means a growing change in our personalities through the work of the Spirit whereby we become more Christlike. As pointed out earlier, these virtues are a description of Jesus.

A few years ago while visiting Boston, I went to Trinity Church where the great preacher Phillips Brooks pastored. It was on a weekday, so I went inside the church and meditated for a few minutes, then quietly slipped under the ropes and mounted Brooks's old pulpit. What a saint he was! Upon leaving the church, I paused outside before the life-sized statue of Brooks standing in his pulpit preaching. The figure of Christ stands beside Brooks, His hand on Brooks's shoulder. The sculptor said that as he studied the great preacher he came to see that the secret of Brooks's life was the indwelling presence of Christ. One day the philosopher Josiah Royce had a student at Harvard ask him, "What is your definition of Christianity?" The philosopher paused, seeking to frame an answer, when at that moment Phillips Brooks passed the study window. "I don't know how to define a Christian . . . but wait—there goes Phillips Brooks!" Would to God the fruit of the Spirit were so developed in all our lives that we, too, could be used as definitions of Christianity!

When the Spirit Is Opposed

All Christians receive the Holy Spirit at conversion. At that time, spiritual gifts are bestowed upon believers. The Holy Spirit wants to produce spiritual fruit in the lives of Christians. In light of these facts, how do we explain those Christians in whose lives there is no evidence of spiritual gifts and no bounty of spiritual fruit? Let's briefly examine two sad verses: "And grieve not the Holy Spirit of God, whereby ye are sealed unto the day of redemption" (Eph. 4:30); and "Quench not the Spirit" (1 Thess. 5:19).

Grieving the Holy Spirit

The grief caused to the Holy Spirit in Ephesians 4:30 has to do with the preceding verse, which warns against evil and filthy speech. We may think of the effects of that grieving of the Spirit in human terms. To grieve the Spirit is to insult and to wound our unseen Companion, Teacher, Comforter, and Guide by our impurity, bitterness, and unforgiveness. Sin not only breaks God's law but also breaks God's heart.

When our sin willfully abounds, the Spirit is grieved. When we grieve the Spirit by word, thought, or deed, He does not leave us, but rather must divert His work. Sin destroys our spirituality, and the Spirit must minister not *through* us, but *to* us in our sinful state.

For us to have truly spiritual lives, ones which are channels for the Spirit, we must deal with our sin on a regular basis. We need to see its reality and danger and recognize our humanity. All of us sin daily, and daily we must confess our sins, taking our courage and assurance from 1 John 1:19: "If we confess our sins, he is faithful and just to forgive us our sins, and to cleanse us from all unrighteousness." Confession is more than just asking for forgiveness; to confess is to pour out in sorrow and repentance before the Almighty God that which we know to be sin.

Quenching the Spirit

The image of quenching the Spirit in 1 Thessalonians 5:19 refers to the following verse, "Despise not prohesyings." Apparently the church in Thessalonica had a tendency to stifle at least some of the gifts of the Spirit. But quenching or stifling of the Spirit by a church, bad as that is, is no worse than individuals quenching the Spirit in their own lives.

How do you and I quench the Spirit in our lives? By our spiritual deafness, by our unreceptiveness to the Spirit's will; by our suspicion or disregard of the methods or ways of the Spirit. Any *unyielding* of our lives to the guiding of the Spirit is a quenching—a no to God.

Our unyielded attitudes actually say more about us than about the Spirit. He does not leave us, nor is His work extinguished. However, our usefulness is quenched. As the glowing coal pulled away from the fire grows cold, so will the spiritual lives of unyielded Christians. In Romans 12:1-2 we have Paul's plea for us to offer our bodies as living sacrifices, our minds being constantly renewed and transformed by yielding to the Spirit and by not conforming to the world.

The Unpardonable Sin Against the Holy Spirit

The Background of This Sin

A chief topic of the Sunday afternoon discussions back when folk invited the preacher over for Sunday dinner was the dreadful possibility of an unpardonable sin. People still wonder about this sin and often link it to sexual sins, divorce, or murder. While none of these is the unpardonable sin, there certainly is an unpardonable sin which can be committed against the Holy Spirit.

The whole idea of such a dreadful sin is rooted in the confrontation of Jesus and the scribes reported in Mark 3:22-30 (see Matt. 12:22-32; Luke 11:14-20). Those religious leaders from Jerusalem maintained that Jesus' power to cast out demons and heal people was from Satan. They said that in spite of clear evidence to the contrary. Jesus denounced their view.

Jesus had little patience with the scribes' assessment of His work, and He gave this stinging rebuke: "Verily I say unto you, all sins shall be forgiven unto the sons of men, and blasphemies wherewith soever they shall blaspheme: But he that shall blaspheme against the Holy [Spirit] hath never forgiveness, but is in danger of eternal damnation." (Mark 3:28-29). Now, the key to interpreting that judgment is in the next statement: "Because they said, He hath an unclean spirit" (v. 30).

Persons are in danger of committing the unpardonable sin against the Holy Spirit when they observe the working of the Holy Spirit of God and declare that it is the work of an unclean spirit, that is, of the devil. The people who spoke with Jesus had been given full opportunity to realize and confess that the miracles of Jesus were of Almighty God, but they stubbornly insisted on saying the Spirit which empowered Jesus was of Satan. In Matthew's account, we see that God understands how people might have had trouble accepting Jesus as the Messiah. He came in the form of man, not God, and ran afoul of the popular ideas of the Coming One. They could have misunderstood Him without deliberate intention: "And whosoever speaketh a word against the Son of man, it shall be forgiven him: but whosoever speaketh a word against the Holy Ghost, it shall not be forgiven him, neither in this world, neither in the world to come" (Matt. 12:32). A person cannot be so blind as not to realize that the power behind Jesus is the Holy Spirit of God.

Why Is This Sin Unpardonable?

Why is the deliberate rejection of the working of the Holy Spirit an unforgivable sin? Because the rejection of the witness of the Spirit to our hearts shuts out the Spirit's convicting and convincing work which would otherwise lead to conversion. Such a rejecting attitude turns the signpost marks leading to heaven around and points them toward hell. This is an unpardonable sin, an unpardonable attitude, because the more we whisper such a lie to ourselves and proclaim it to others, the harder our hearts become and the more spiritually blind we become. Blind fish deep in caves are fish which could once see, but because they have swum in the dark recesses of the cave for a long time their eyes have become useless and no longer function. So it is with people who call the darkness light and the light darkness. Finally they will reach a place where truth and lie seem the same; they lose the ability to distinguish the right from the wrong, the good from the bad. Such people will not come to God. Such people make themselves unpardonable since they reject the means of pardon.

The other side of this coin is that some sensitive Christians, whose hearts and lives are tuned to the Holy Spirit, worry about this sin. Hear this well: If you are so anxious to please our Lord that you worry about commiting this sin, there is *no chance at all* that you are in danger of committing the unpardonable sin. Your very desire to be open to His guidance is insurance against your being guilty of such a sin.

Notes

1. Dale Moody, *Spirit of the Living God* (Philadelphia: The Westminster Press, 1968), p. 93.

2. Ibid., p. 95.

3. W. A. Criswell, *The Holy Spirit in Today's World* (Grand Rapids: Zondervan Publishing House, 1966), pp. 192-93.

4. Frank Stagg, *The Holy Spirit Today,* p. 68.

5. Handley C. G. Moule, *The Epistle to the Romans* (Grand Rapids: Zondervan, n.d.), p. 325.

6. L. H. Marshall, *The Challenge of New Testament Ethics* (London: MacMillan and Co., Ltd., 1950), p. 293.

7. William Wordsworth, "Peter Bell: A Tale" in Walford Davies, ed., *William Wordsworth: Selected Poems* (London: J. M. Dent and Sons Limited, 1975), p. 100.

7

The Direction
When Is the Church Really
the Church?

A famous scholar posed this question, "When is the Church really the Church?" Certainly not when it turns its face toward the past and ignores the present and future, for to do that imprisons the church in tradition. Certainly the church is not really the church when it cuts itself completely loose from the past and casts itself into every whim and wave of modern thought, for that way leads to heresy. The church is truly what God intends it to be when it is guided by the Holy Spirit.[1]

The church is truly the church when it realizes it is the church of the Spirit. Just as Jesus was supremely guided and filled by the Spirit, so the early church was filled and guided by that same Spirit (See Luke and Acts). The reality of the church shows the vitality and reign of the Holy Spirit. The Holy Spirit is not the spirit of the church, but the Spirit of God; that means the church is answerable to the Spirit and created by the Spirit. In a famous sermon on the Holy Spirit, Augustine said, "What the soul is for the body of a man, that is what the Holy Spirit is for the body of Christ, which is the Church; what the soul works in all the members of the body, that the Spirit works in the whole of the church."[2] The Spirit, then, is the soul of the church, and as such He is free, creative, and has authority to give gifts, bring peace, and rebuke the church. The Spirit animates and makes alive the church, and so He is to the church as breath is to the body.

The Spirit Creates the Church

The church universal, and its local expressions in every community as churches, is created not by the whim of man nor the will of the flesh, not by human invention nor happenstance, but by the Spirit. In most of the ancient creeds of the church the order is the Spirit, then the church, then the communion (fellowship) of the saints, and forgiveness.

The Church as the Body

The Spirit creates the church, as Acts 2 so powerfully portrays. The most vivid picture of the church is that of a *body*. This image is used in the New Testament in two ways: Christ as the body, and we as Christians as the various parts of the body. "For as the body is one, and hath many members, and all the members of that one body, being many, are one body: so also is Christ" (1 Cor. 12:12). Paul was describing the local church in terms of its gifts, saying that the many gifted Christians who make up the church are all together forming the church, the body of Christ.

The fullest and clearest expression of the Spirit-created body is found in Ephesians, where Christ is spoken of as the head of the body, the church. Paul prayed that we may "grow up into him in all things, which is the head, even Christ: From whom the whole body fitly joined together and compacted by that which every joint supplieth, according to the effectual working in the measure of every part" (Eph. 4:15-16). The same clear image of the Spirit-led church as Christ's body is seen in Ephesians 1:22-23: "and gave him to be the head over all things to the church, Which is his body, the fulness of him that filleth all in all."

The Church as the Temple

The holy place.—A second image stressing the relationship of the Spirit to the church is that of a temple. There are three primary passages of Scripture which reveal the work of the Spirit in this regard: 1 Corinthians 3:16-17; Ephesians 2:18-22; and 1 Peter 2:5. The Corinthian passage bluntly raises the question: "Know ye not that ye are the temple of God, and that the Spirit of God dwelleth in you?" The emphasis in this passage is upon the church as the holy place of God, indwelt by the Holy Spirit. To defile the temple of God—and I take this to be a reference to the collective local church congregation at Corinth—is to risk personal punishment by God.

The living stones.—The Ephesian passage speaks of the Spirit giving access to the Father through Jesus' sacrifice and proclaims that even foreigners—Gentiles—are made part of God's household. We become a part of the holy temple to the Lord, Jesus being the chief cornerstone and we the other living stones. This spiritual building, fitting together perfectly (which speaks of unity and fellowship), becomes through the Spirit a holy home for God.

The royal priesthood.—In 1 Peter 2 the idea of our being living stones from which the spiritual house of God is constructed continues but is linked to another liturgical image—the sacrificial system. In keeping with the Old Testament sacrificial practices, priests are needed to bring the offerings before God, and this is set forth in this passage as a work of the church. The offerings are spiritual and consist of our prayers, our gathered worship, our lives and witness and ministry. We are, as Peter said, a "royal priesthood" (v. 9).

The Spirit as Protector of the Church

Not only is each Christian the temple of the Spirit, but also the entire local church and, indeed, the church universal, is a spiritual temple indwelt by the Holy Spirit. The church is the place, above all, of the presence of the Spirit. In this role, the Spirit is the guarantee of the purity of the church. We read in 1 Corinthians 12 that only by the Holy Spirit can anyone call Jesus Lord. Any utterance at variance with the deity of Jesus is by an imposter, not guided by the Spirit. As we ponder the work of the Spirit in creating the body of Christ, the temple of God in the Spirit, and in the work of defending the purity of the church, we must raise a question: Do we as Christians, and as churches, place far too much emphasis on the physical building and not nearly enough on the spiritual nature of the church of which we are part?

The Spirit Places the Christian in the Church

The Holy Spirit brings each believer into the church through the baptism of the Spirit, "For by one Spirit are we all baptized into one body" (1 Cor. 12:13). There is no entrance to the church except by the Spirit's baptism. This inward baptism is symbolized by the outward water baptism to which we joyfully submit.

The church into which we are placed by the Spirit is not easily seen. Each local church is but the tip of the great iceberg, as it were, of the larger church which shall one day gather before the throne of God. The true church is smaller than our church records show, and greater than all our church rolls!

The Spirit Endows the Church

As stated earlier, every Christian is given at least one spiritual gift for the upbuilding of the local church. To use our spiritual gifts properly is to use them to worship and minister in the Holy Spirit as part of the church. By endowing the individual Christian, the Spirit is endowing the church. The body of Christ as a gifted body is most adequately expressed in Ephesians 4. The gifts affect the church's edification, worship, ministry, and witness.

The Spirit Bestows Unity and Fellowship

The Unity of the Church

The words of Baring-Gould's hymn are quite right:

> We are not divided;
> All one body we,
> One in hope and doctrine
> One in charity.[3]

It may seem that Christendom is sorely divided by its many denominations and sects, yet we all believe the earliest confession of faith: Jesus is Lord! How marvelous it would be if all Christians could both speak and act out of the truth of the statement: "In things essential, unity; in things not essential, charity."

The Holy Spirit is both the Creator and Keeper of the essential unity of the church. The gifts are to be seen in light of this unity, as they result in the perfection of saints for ministry, in the edifying of the body of Christ, and in drawing all its members toward the essential unity God intends for the church (Eph. 4:13). Discord is both a threat to the unity of the local congregation and a challenge to the Spirit. This is illustrated in the issue of eating meat offered to idols, discussed in Paul in several passages. "But if thy brother be grieved with thy meat, now walkest thou not charitably. Destroy not him with thy meat, for whom Christ died. Let not then your good be evil spoken of: For the kingdom of God is not meat and drink, but righteousness, and peace, and joy in the Holy Ghost" (Romans 14:15-17). The testimony continues in 1 Corinthians 8: "Wherefore, if meat make my brother to offend, I will eat no flesh while the world standeth, lest I make my brother to offend" (v. 13).

From prison Paul appealed to the Philippian church to preserve the unity in the Spirit:

> If there be therefore any consolation in Christ, if any comfort of love, if any fellowship of the spirit, if any bowels and mercies, Fulfil ye my joy, that ye be like-minded, having the same love, being of one accord, of one mind. Let nothing be done through strife or vainglory; but in lowliness of mind let each esteem other better than themselves. Look not every man on his own things, but every man also on the things of others (Phil. 2:1-4).

Unity of the Spirit is grounded in the sevenfold statement of unity found in Ephesians 4:4-6: "There is one body, and one Spirit, even as ye are called in one hope of your calling; One Lord, one faith, one baptism. One God and Father of all, who is above all, and through all, and in you all."

The Fellowship of the Church

The unity of the church under the Spirit shows itself in fellowship, a caring spirit toward the people of God. In the first church, we see the members sharing with one another (Acts 4:34-35). Barnabas was singled out as an example of the love and unity and fellowship created by the Spirit (vv. 36-37). We also see the challenge to the Spirit created by disunity and wrong motives within the church when Ananias and Sapphira pretended to follow the example of Barnabas in selling their land but giving only part: "But Peter said, Ananias, why hath Satan filled thine heart to lie to the Holy Ghost, and to keep back part of the price of the land?" (Acts 5:3). To pretend to be part of the unity and fellowship of the church when we are not is to sin not only against our fellow church members but also against the Holy Spirit.

The nature of the fellowship created by the Spirit is different from that created by people and by the devil. "It shall not be so among you." This eternal fellowship is more than just the pull of good people toward each other or the comradeship of a civic club. We do not *choose* each other in the church; we are chosen of God and placed in a relationship of fellowship, *koinonia,* by the Spirit. Our "familyness" is not ended when we see things differently—we are still brothers and sisters in Christ, possessors of an otherworldly unity and fellowship. This fellowship builds through shared worship and witness.

One of the most beautiful illustrations of the unity and fellowship the

Holy Spirit creates in the church happened a few years ago in the church I pastor. Two small boys, one white and one black, were sitting together in church. The little black lad's mother sang in the choir—the only black lady in the choir. The little white boy's mother selected a seat behind the boys. As they began to whisper during the service, the white lad's mother leaned over with a word of correction to the boys. A moment later the black boy asked his friend, "Who's she?" "That's my mother," was the whispered reply. "My mother is in the choir," said the little black boy—to which his friend responded, "Which one is she?" May the Spirit make us all more colorblind as we experience more of God's grace together!

The fellowship of the Spirit is beautifully spelled out in John 17 and 1 John 1. In the first passage Jesus, in the high priestly prayer, prayed for Himself, for His twelve disciples, and for those who would come to believe in Him through the ages (see especially vv. 20-26).

First John 1 declares that the driving force behind the proclamation of the Gospel is that "ye also may have fellowship with us: and truly our fellowship is with the Father, and with his Son Jesus Christ" (v. 3). This passage also spells out that thing which destroys fellowship: "If we say that we have fellowship with him, and walk in darkness, we lie, and do not the truth" (v. 6). The life of consecration leads to fellowship: "If we walk in the light, as he is in the light, we have fellowship one with another, and the blood of Jesus Christ his Son cleanses us from all sin" (v. 7).

The Spirit as Worship Leader

Many of our churches are either very dignified, stiff, and formal or are extremely emotional and have trouble sitting still during the worship service. Heaven forbid that we must take only one of these positions as our worship model! We must admit that the apostles were thought to be drunk when they preached on the Day of Pentecost, and Spirit-led worship is most surely compared to being drunk in Ephesians 5:18 which describes gathered worship, "Be not drunk with wine, wherein is excess; but be filled with the Spirit." Yet the Holy Spirit is also the author of order in worship, as we see in Paul's discussion about tongue speaking and prophesying in the Corinthian church: "For God is not the author of confusion, but of peace, as in all churches of the saints" (1 Cor. 14:33).

For most churches, "the chief modern heresy in worship concerning the Holy Spirit is the neglect of His presence and power."[4] For while there is a real danger in letting our worship experiences run wild emotionally, the Holy Spirit is no more responsible for that unhelpful and divisive behavior than He is for the cold, emotionless communion with self which characterizes some other worship experiences! If we expect and look for the presence of the Spirit in our services of worship, we can approach those hours of worship with a genuine sense of expectancy. Something greater and deeper than merely what is written on the order of service is going to happen.

We should have great variety in our worship format, but we should always remember that we are dependent upon the Spirit to inbreathe reality and life to worship. True worship under the guidance of the Spirit calls forth spiritual gifts to enrich the service—gifts of singing, preaching, teaching, and praise.

The Singing Church

Singing and praising ought to be a vital part of worship services, for we are specifically commanded to worship in song, "Speaking to yourselves in psalms and hymns and spiritual songs, singing and making melody in your heart to the Lord" (Eph. 5:19). But it is not music for music's sake or music to educate the congregation musically that is admonished here. Paul was encouraging the expression of joyful, grateful, blood-bought and Spirit-led salvation experiences which bubble over into worship of Almighty God. In the beautiful picture of worship around the heavenly throne of God in Revelation 5, we see all creation singing as they worship, singing a new song of praise to the Lamb.

The Praying Church

Prayer is another Spirit-led element of worship. In both private and public prayer, the Holy Spirit plays an important role. In Romans 8:26-27 we are told that the Spirit prays for us when we do not know what to say. And it is implied that the Spirit does this for the gathered church as well. The Spirit is not only the initiator of prayer but is also manifest as a result of prayer. In Acts we read, "when they had prayed, the place was shaken where they were assembled together; and they were all filled with the Holy Ghost" (4:31).

We are given a promise concerning prayer in Matthew 18:19: "Again I say unto you, that if two of you shall *agree*" (author's italics). The Greek word translated *agree* comes from *sumphōneō* from which we get the word *symphony*. The Spirit-led prayer of the church is a symphony of voices and hearts blending in beautiful unity and agreement with each other and God. From its very birth, the true church has ever been a praying church under the guidance of the Spirit.

The Preaching Church

In the Protestant tradition, the sermon holds a dominant place in the worship service. As the Spirit guides in the congregation's expressions of praise in song and in its communion with the Father in prayer, so also is the Spirit to be in control of the proclamation of the gospel. The Spirit creates in the minds of the worshipers a sense of the presence of God, a sense that within the spoken words are personal words from God for them, words greater than the words and the preacher. Often the Spirit uses some word or thought in a manner never intended by the preacher. An unforgettable illustration is that of the man finally converted after years of attending preaching services. When he was asked by the minister what it was in that sermon which finally got through to him, the man replied, "It was when you said, 'Now let us leave the first part of the sermon, and go on to the next part.' It was then I realized it was time for me to have done with the first part of my life and go on to the next part by conversion!"

Spirit-filled proclamation is a mark of the church. Paul spoke of its value in 1 Corinthians, and the Jerusalem church found itself preaching with boldness and convicting power under the Spirit when Peter and John healed the lame man at the Temple in Acts 3. When they used the crowd which gathered as an opportunity to witness, the Spirit gave them power and wisdom to speak. When they were imprisoned for preaching, they were questioned by the religious leaders who noted both their preaching power and lack of formal knowledge and said of them that they had been with Jesus. What the priests did not realize was that the disciples' fellowship with Jesus was not a thing of the past only, but a continuing presence through the Holy Spirit.

The Spirit and the Ordinances

Of supreme importance to most churches are the ordinances of baptism and the Lord's Supper. In both the presence and leadership of the Holy Spirit is prominent.

Baptism and the Spirit

According to the Synoptic Gospels, neither Jesus nor His disciples baptized, nor did He give a command to do such until His postresurrection ministry. Yet there apparently was never a time when the church did not baptize. The reasons are to be found in the example of Jesus' baptism and the coming of the Spirit as a dove upon Him at that time. We also remember the words of John the Baptist that Jesus would baptize with the Holy Spirit; and we are mindful of the command of Jesus concerning baptism before His ascension and the powerful outpouring of the Holy Spirit on the disciples at Pentecost. In this event, they saw the fulfillment of the promise of baptism with the Spirit.

The water baptism of the church is prophetic symbolism, that is, an acting out of the death, burial, and resurrection of the believer with Christ and an affirming of the baptism of each of us in the Holy Spirit. Thus the words are spoken in baptism: "I baptize thee, my [brother/sister], in the name of the Father, and the Son, and the Holy Spirit." In itself baptism has no saving power; yet it is not an empty symbol, for the Holy Spirit is acting in this ordinance to stamp upon our lives the significance of our entrance into the body of Christ. Baptism stands at the beginning of the Christian life and is the doorway into the church.

The Lord's Supper and the Spirit

The second ordinance is the Lord's Supper. This sacred event is repeated many times in a Christian's life, while baptism is intended to be experienced only once. The supper consists of the eating of bread and the drinking of wine or grape juice. There is no change in the bread or the fruit of the vine; they are simply physical representations of the body and blood of Christ. The supper is a time when we feel the presence of the Holy Spirit in a deep and moving way. At the table of the Lord, we join with other Christians in a time of spiritual recollection as we are made to mediate through the bread and fruit of the vine on our Lord's death and our death with him. We celebrate the presence of our risen Lord and remember that as long as we gather at His table we show forth His death until He returns (1 Cor. 11:26). Our gathering at the Lord's table is also a token of our future communion and joy in heaven, as we remember the promises scattered throughout Scripture that the righteous shall feast with the Messiah in the world to come and as we mediate on Jesus' promise to feast with His disciples in the Kingdom.

Our celebration of both these ordinances is under the guidance of the Holy spirit and in His presence. We marvel when we think on the simple but moving act of baptism as the believer is immersed in water. We marvel when we reflect that in these nearly two thousand years since our Lord asked His disciples to "do this in remembrance of me" not a Sunday has gone by without Christians gathering at the Lord's table somewhere in this world! The Lord's Supper is the Lord's song in a foreign land (see Ps. 137).

Over and over through the inward testimony of the Holy Spirit, we interpret our faith. We celebrate these ordinances in the presence of other Christians; the shared act of commitment and remembrance with our brothers and sisters in Christ makes both of these ordinances *church* ordinances. They express our fellowship with each other through the Holy Spirit.

The Spirit and the Mission of the Church

"The Spirit does not just keep the Church going; He keeps it going out into the world with the Gospel."[5] The Holy Spirit gives the church guidance for understanding its existence and purpose; He empowers it for the task; He gives a sense of urgency to the mission; He rebukes the church when its memory grows dim.

The Guiding Spirit

The hand and heart behind the church, guiding it across the centuries, is the Holy Spirit. This is clearly seen in the first recorded meeting of the churches as the church in what is known as the Jerusalem Conference of Acts 15. We read in verse 28 that "it seemed good to the Holy [Spirit], and to us, to lay upon you no greater burdens" The Spirit would not allow the church to merely be a sect of Judaism, and the Holy Spirit today will not allow the church to be the servant of nationalism or culture.

The Spirit guides not only the universal church in its mission but also the local church and the individual Christian. He sets overseers over the churches (Acts 20:28), and those among us who fill that role as pastors must ever be careful to seek the Spirit's guidance.

This guidance of the Spirit gives the church boldness. A leading characteristic of the first Christians was boldness, courage. The authorities took note of the boldness of Peter and John, and apparently they and all the Christians in times of harrassment and persecution were able to give a reasoned account of the hope within them. This is fulfillment of Jesus' promise that they were not to worry about what to say when hauled before the authorities: "For the Holy [Spirit] shall teach you in the same hour what ye ought to say" (Luke 12:12).

The Missionary Spirit

A widening circle of evangelism is directed by the Holy Spirit in the New Testament. Evangelism's power and directions are the work of the Spirit: "But ye shall receive power, after that the Holy [Spirit] is come upon you: and ye shall be witnesses unto me both in Jerusalem, and in all Judaea, and in Samaria, and unto the uttermost part of the earth" (Acts 1:8).

The Spirit directs individuals concerning where to witness. He sent Philip to meet the Ethiopian eunuch on the desert road to Gaza (Acts 8:26,29,39). He sent Peter to Cornelius (Acts 10:19-20). He separated Paul and Barnabas from the church in Antioch (Acts 13:2) and sent them forth. The Spirit gave direct guidance as to where Paul was to preach, turning him away from certain areas and sending him to others (Acts 16:6-10). So we see the Spirit selecting the missionary, sending the missionary, and preparing the hearts of those to whom he would preach.

For a church to be a vital, living church, it must be a witnessing church. There must be an excitement, an enthusiasm, a burden for lost souls. "No heart is pure that is not passionate; no virtue is safe that is not enthusiastic," so an old saying goes. This necessary sense of compassion, compulsion, and urgency is of the Spirit: "For we cannot but speak the things which we have seen and heard" (Acts 4:20).

The Rebuking Spirit

Since we are frail and imperfect, having our treasure in earthern vessels, the Spirit also exercises a disciplinary role. An instance of the rebuke of the Spirit which was, no doubt, long remembered by the church at Antioch was the sharp rebuke the Spirit delivered through Paul to Peter. Paul "withstood him to the face, because he was to be blamed. For before that certain came from James, he did eat with the Gentiles: but when they were come, he withdrew and separated himself, fearing them which were of the circumcision" (Gal. 2:11-12; see also vv. 13-16). Paul realized that such action as that of Peter and Barnabas was contrary to what the Spirit had commanded earlier at the Jerusalem Conference.

Perhaps the most painful rebuke of the Spirit recorded in the New Testament is that given through Paul to the church at Corinth. In 1 Corinthians, Paul taught the beautiful doctrine of the individual and the church as temples, dwelling places of the Spirit. Then he had to turn around and rebuke them as the Spirit's mouthpiece: "What will ye? shall I come to you with a rod, or in love, or in the spirit of meekness?" (4:21). He went on to rebuke the church for condoning sexual immorality in their midst and commanded them to exclude the guilty party. In 2 Corinthians the person guilty of sexual immorality repented and was restored to the fellowship of the church.

The Book of Revelation gives us a vivid picture of the rebuking work of the Spirit. In chapters 2 and 3 are found the letters to the seven churches of Asia Minor. Each letter concludes with an admonition to hear what the Spirit is saying to the churches. A reading of these letters will show that only the churches of Smyrna and Philadelphia escaped the rebuke of the Spirit for coldness of spirit, for spiritual blindness and poverty, and for compromise with evil. "He that hath an ear, let him hear what the Spirit saith unto the churches" (see chs. 2—3).

Notes

1. Hans Küng, *The Church,* pp. 12-13.

2. Augustine quoted in Hendrikus Berkhof, *The Doctrine of the Holy Spirit* (Richmond: John Knox Press, 1964), p. 42.

3. Sabine Baring-Gould, "Onward, Christian Soldiers."

4. Franklin Segler, *Christian Worship* (Nashville: Broadman Press, 1967), p. 63.

5. John Peck, *What the Bible Teaches About the Holy Spirit,* p. 76.

8

The Defiant Life
Is There Victory Over the Devil?

A mighty fortress is our God, A bulwark never failing;
Our helper he, amid the flood Of mortal ills prevailing,
For still our ancient foe Doth seek to work us woe;
His craft and power are great, And, armed with cruel hate,
On earth is not his equal.

. . . .

The Spirit and the gifts are ours
Thro' Him who with us sideth;
Let goods and kindred go, This mortal life also;
The body they may kill; God's truth abideth still,
His kingdom is forever.[1]

The Reality of Satan

Not long ago I was visiting the "Pink Palace," a Memphis museum. I had paid my admission fee when, sensing movement behind me, I turned to see a triceratops—a huge dinosaur with three horns and a mean look—take a menacing, noisy step toward me with a lowered head. The floor shook when he set his foot down! To be honest, I lived a panic-stricken split second before realizing it was a clever mechanical mock-up of the monster. It was worth the price of the museum admission just to watch the reaction of the children to this beast. A quarter placed in a slot on a nearby post brought the creature to life for a few snorts and a stomp or two. Yet the dinosaur is not real.

But Satan is, and the tragedy is that too many Christians act as if he were not. We do not get such an attitude from the Bible. Every New Testament writer, without exception, referred to the devil or demonic powers. The evil dimension of the powers of darkness is no mere superstition, no veneer of the first century; it is at the heart of the New Testament story. Jesus certainly believed in the devil and struggled with him all through His ministry. If our Lord accepted the reality of the devil, then surely if we deny or ignore him, we do it to our hurt.

The Unity of Satan's Dominion

The devil and his cohorts are called by a multitude of names in the New Testament, such as the devil, Satan, spirit of wickedness, thrones, angels, demons, prince of the powers of the air, the destroyer, and the god of this world. These various names show that the biblical writers were not concerned with what they called the devil and his horde—all these represent *one* kingdom headed by one being, the devil. They were concerned with the reality of Satan. The power of evil is a single force under the control of Satan, and Satan's goal is the complete destruction of every person in every way. That kind of enemy frightens me.

Satan's Opposition to Jesus

Jesus struggled a lifetime with Satan. At the Last Supper He said of the disciples: "Ye are they which have continued with me in my temptations" (Luke 22:28). The temptations at the beginning of Jesus' ministry were a test of strength which showed the devil to be the weaker of the two. Satan then left Jesus "for a season" (Luke 4:13). The various encounters with demons were of Satan, and we read that the devil even got into the inner circle of disciples: "Then entered Satan into Judas, . . . being of the number of the twelve" (Luke 22:3). Satan obtained the power to sift Peter and would no doubt have succeeded, but for the prayers of Jesus (vv. 31-32). To the soldiers who came to the garden to arrest Him, Jesus said, "This is your hour, and the power of darkness" (v. 53).

Jesus' death on the cross struck at the very stronghold of Satan and defeated him. The resurrection is the ultimate proof of Christ's victory over the devil. A great spiritual battle has raged in heaven and on earth since the birth of Christ. The lesson from Luke 10:18; 1 Peter 3:19; and Revelation 12, having to do with Hades and Satan, is that through the work of Jesus, Satan lost any toehold in heaven; the harsh reality for us is that now that great dragon, that serpent, the deceiver of the whole world, is cast down to the earth. Here he roams the world like a hungry lion (1 Pet. 5:8-10), making war on the brothers and sisters of Christ (Rev.

12:12,17). No especially spiritual, especially endowed group of "green-beret" Christians carry on this warfare while the rest relax; the entire church is involved.

Satan's Opposition to Every Christian

Our study of life in the Spirit would be incomplete if we ignored that dark opposition, that spiritual enemy, we call Satan! We Christians are in a war! At the battle of Bull Run during the Civil War, the high society of Washington came out to watch the Union Army obliterate the rebels and found themselves being peppered with gunfire! Christians who think the struggle with Satan is a similarly amusing Sunday afternoon outing may find themselves likewise in the midst of battle! For, in Bunyan's words, there are always "archers standing ready in Beelzebub's Castle to shoot them who should knock at the wicket-gate for entrance."[2]

Several things we must remember in our spiritual warfare. We must remember that we could not dare to do battle with Satan if he were not *already* ultimately defeated, if he were not even now crippled. The invasion of Satan's kingdom has already taken place in Jesus' ministry, and the decisive battle was won on the cross; we are in the mopping-up action. A second thing to remember is that our spiritual battle is not against flesh and blood, but against unseen spiritual powers of evil, who, even when seen, may appear as angels of light (Eph. 6:12). A third truth which we must ever keep in mind is that the devil knows he only has a short time (Rev. 12:12), and that fact enrages him.

The Christian's Battle with Satan

A few years ago, one of my church members, in an encounter with a patrolman, made a comment I'll never forget. The patrolman "pulled her over" on the main street, and that in itself is embarrassing enough, but especially to this genteel, Southern-drawling lady. And it didn't help for the pastor to come by just then and wave broadly at her and the policeman! Later she told me her angry response to the policeman for stopping her for speeding: "Why, you ought to be ashamed of yourself, arresting fine ladies like me! You ought to be out there after the criminals!" That illustrates our idea that Satan ought let us good folk alone! But Satan has declared war on each of us who belong to Jesus.

Paul's Images

Our hymnals are full of military images to describe Christian life: "Stand Up for Jesus, Ye Soldiers of the Cross," "Onward, Christian Soldiers," "Am I a Soldier of the Cross," "My Soul, Be on Thy Guard," "Fight the Good Fight," "A Mighty Fortress Is Our God," just to name a few. Paul baptized the images of war and used them effectively. He told the Roman Christians to put on the armor of light and, writing to the Ephesians, enumerated the various items of the Christian soldier's armor. In the Second Letter to the Corinthians, Paul said that, though the weapons of our warfare are not carnal, they are, nevertheless, mighty through God to the pulling down of strongholds—the strongholds of sin and of the devil. In 1 Corinthians Paul compared himself to a soldier and claimed the right to live by the gospel, just as a soldier lives at the expense of those for whom he fights. In the Epistle to the Philippians, Epaphroditus is called Paul's "fellowsoldier"; and similar expressions are found in the Letters of Timothy and in the Second Letter to the Corinthians. To Timothy, Paul said: "Thou therefore endure hardness as a good soldier of Jesus Christ" (2 Tim. 2:3), and added that no man, being a soldier to God, entangles himself with secular affairs. Military language came naturally to Paul. In fact, we can say that any Christian writer who wishes to employ the image of the spiritual soldier need look no further for an example than the writings of Paul."[3]

The Soldier, the Army, the Kingdom

Behind the individual soldier in any battle is the larger unity of which he is a part. The Japanese soldiers who until recently were hiding out on the islands of the Pacific are simply strange curiosities—cavedwellers who hid away from civilization nearly forty years—if we separate them from their identity as part of the Japanese army which fought a life-and-death struggle in 1945. The individual soldier represents and gets his meaning from the army to which he belongs. Behind the army is the country or kingdom for which it fights. So our struggle against the devil is a struggle between two kingdoms.

Matthew 12 provides a vivid picture of the two kingdoms at war in human affairs. The Pharisees thought Jesus did His mighty works through the power of Beelzebub, the prince of the devils. Jesus' reply was, "Every kingdom divided against itself is brought to desolation . . . if Satan cast out Satan, . . . how shall then his kingdom stand?" (v. 25-26). "But if I cast out devils by the Spirit of God, then the kingdom of God is come unto you" (v. 28). The battle is God's kingdom against Satan's kingdom.

Satan's kingdom is this present world, twisted and broken by sin. His goal is to tempt people and institutions to rebel against God, to distort the truth of God's love, and to enslave people. The seriousness and severity of Satan's corrupting rule in the world is seen in Paul's First Letter to the Corinthians. As Paul addressed the problem of a man openly living an immoral life, he urged the church to "deliver such an one unto Satan for the destruction of the flesh" (5:5). By this he apparently meant to withdraw Christian fellowship from the man, to treat him as an unbeliever, to take from him the comfort and guidance of the church. They were to thrust him back into the world where, in the midst of moral corruption and hopelessness, he might feel isolated and separated from God's love and surrounded by the hellish hopelessness of Satan's world and come to his senses. The world outside the church is dominated by Satan.

But the soldier has not only the assurance that he is part of an army which carries the banner of the kingdom of God against the kingdom of Satan but also has the powerful presence of the Holy Spirit to help him defeat the devil. Remember Paul's fine statement of the exchanged life in Galatians 2:20: "yet not I, but Christ liveth in me." That is the note which sounds above the conflict. The unceasing struggle against the spirit of Antichrist, which was raging in the days of the disciple John and yet continues, has the sure outcome of victory because "greater is he that is in you, than he that is in the world" (1 John 4:4).

The Weapons of Our Warfare

Satan's Sword: Temptation

Just how does the devil make war on us, and what spiritual weapons shall we use in standing against him? The devil attacks us both as individuals and as churches. Temptation is the specific weapon of the devil, and he builds on the marriage that "the grass in greener on the other side." But the best he can actually offer us is a counterfeit crown, phony power, and ultimate ruin. A study of Paul's letters will show us how serious is the tempter's power, as Paul feared his work with the Thessalonians might have been in vain due to Satan's tempting (1 Thess. 3:5). Paul the bachelor warned how the devil tempts us sexually (1 Cor. 7:5). Even the candidate for bishop must be aware of the snare of the devil (1 Tim. 3:7).

From the biblical warnings, we can know we are making progress in spiritual growth if we are the target of the devil's darts of temptation. To feel no temptation may mean that Satan already has his way in our daily lives and that we are not worth his attention and energy. In that case he has destroyed our witness for Christ. A lack of feeling temptation may mean that we have been so lulled and deadened by the devil so that we do not feel his terrible onslaught when it comes. As a rule, however, those who seek a close walk with the Lord will feel the brunt of the devil's temptation.

The comment of the author of a thirteenth-century religious manual is so true:

> Let no one of holy life think that she will not be tempted. The good, who have climbed high, are more greatly tempted than the weak. And this is to be expected, for the higher the hill the more the wind blows about it. The higher the hill of holy, exalted life, the more and the stronger will be the Devil's blasts and the winds of temptation.[4]

Usually the seasoned saint seems unaware of having achieved some measure of victory over the devil; she is more aware of her weakness and need for the power of the Holy Spirit.

The most seductive and effective temptations of Satan are not the sins of the flesh. True, these have traditionally been seen as most serious and have led us almost to idolize purity from fleshly sins. We should be aware of the power of the flesh, but we must not ignore sins of the heart and mind. We have these three—the world, the flesh, and the devil—and while the devil is behind both, the lust of the world, and the lust for fame and fortune and self-trust is equally evil and damning.

To Withstand Temptation

How shall we withstand temptations and live victorious lives in Christ and over Satan? We find three vital words on this challenge in the New Testament: *blood, witness,* and *armor.*

The blood of the lamb.—"And they overcame him by the blood of the Lamb, and by the word of their testimony" (Rev. 12:11). We cannot hope to withstand Satan in our own strength, nor must we; we have been cleansed of our sins by the blood of Christ. In the spiritual power released in Christ's death and resurrection and bestowed upon us, we can defeat Satan. The cheapened use of the cross in vampire movies to ward off evil is a caricature of the fact that the blood of Jesus, applied to our lives in salvation, truly is effective in keeping Satan at bay.

Testimony.—The Book of Revelation says we overcome Satan by our testimonies. Psalm 34:1-7 is a beautiful statement of the value of a person's testimony of the presence, forgiveness, and goodness of the Lord. In Revelation 12:11 we read that our testimonies not only give us strength and comfort but also overcome Satan. The word *testimony* here is the same word as *martyr,* and we know that often the early Christians sealed their testimonies—their witness—with death. Reflecting on our testimonies and sharing them when proper are, indeed, powerful tools in resisting Satan.

Armor.—The third concept in defeating Satan, along with blood and witness, is armor. The classic passage dealing with our spiritual armor is Ephesians 6:10-18. The warlike image is due to the seriousness with which Paul treated the devil's "wiles." Our struggles are not long-range and impersonal, but hand-to-hand battles. In this verse Paul warned that our battles are spiritual and that we need spiritual armor. The pieces of armor represent realities of spiritual life: truth (the glorious truth about God, about Christ, and about man), righteousness (which is not of man, but of God), the gospel of peace (the good news of peace from God, with God, and of God), faith (saving faith and mountain-moving faith), salvation (which will reorient our lives), and the Word of God (both the spoken and written word).

The armor is for protection and as such enables us to move offensively for Christ. As is so often pointed out, this armor offers no protection for our backs—we are not to turn our backs to our spiritual enemy but to press onward against him. The sword of the Spirit is certainly an offensive weapon. Paul seemed to underline faith in verse 16: "Above all, talking the shield of faith, wherewith ye shall be able to quench all the fiery darts of the wicked." The darts—arrows dipped in pitch and set aflame—are the temptations of the devil.

We are bidden to put on this armor with prayer: unceasing, deep, and fervent prayer through the Holy Spirit; prayer at all times: all kinds of prayer; and all the church praying. Prayer is our link to the spiritual power which is rightly ours in Christ. Along with prayer, we are urged to be sober and vigilant since our enemy is like a roaring lion (1 Pet. 5:8). This soberness is an attitude of reality about ourselves, our world, and the devil. To be sober is to be free from the illusions of sin.

We are also told to test the spirits, for not all those who pretend to speak by and for God really belong to Him (1 John 4:1 and 1 Cor. 14:1). Even the devil can dress himself as an angel of light (2 Cor. 11:14). Part of our struggle, and our pilgrimage toward spiritual maturity, is the testing of the spirits within our lives and the lives of others.

A final injunction is to avoid situations of temptation—"Abstain from all appearance of evil" (1 Thess. 5:22). Do not be used of Satan to tempt others to sin nor willingly place yourself in a position of spiritual weakness.

The image of Christians making their spiritual stand, girded in the armor of the Holy Spirit, watchful and wielding the Sword of the Spirit is a grand picture! Not half-hearted, discouraged Christians, but ones whose warfare, though carried out on our knees, is filled with the trumpets of the morning and the reward of the Savior in whose power we conquer our age-old enemy.

> "I am going to my Father's; and though with great difficulty I have got hither, yet now I do not repent me of all the trouble I have been at to arrive where I am. My sword I give to him that shall succeed me in my pilgrimage, and my courage and skill to him that can get it. My marks and scars I carry with me, to be a witness for me that I have fought His battles who will now be my rewarder." . . . So he passed over, and the trumpets sounded for him on the other side.[5]

Notes

1. Martin Luther, "A Mighty Fortress Is Our God."
2. John Bunyan, *The Pilgrim's Progress*, p. 267.
3. See Gerald Bonner, *The Warfare of Christ*, p. 40.
4. Ibid., pp. 100-101.
5. Bunyan, p. 281.

9

The Destiny
Tell Me Again About
The Promised Victory

We are given a promise and possibility of victory in our daily struggles with the devil; yet an even greater and eternal victory will be ours through the Holy Spirit at the close of this world.

Salvation is a past fact, justification; a present process, sanctification; and a future consummation, redemption. So we see that the presence of the Holy Spirit in Christian lives leads not only to a realization of the separation from this present world but also to a strong assurance of victory and the glories of the world to come.

Final Victory Through the Spirit

The word *victory* in the New Testament is connected with the Holy Spirit, from Jesus' victory over the devil by the Spirit of God (Matt. 12:28) to the words of our Lord as John saw Him presiding over the new Jerusalem and saying to the victorious Christians: "He that overcometh shall inherit all things; and I will be his God, and he shall be my son" (Rev. 21:7). In Revelation 21:7 we see the tension of the victory—present in daily life but also not yet present in its fullness. We are children of God already and yet children to be. The future victory and the promised inheritance are both the result of sonship which is ours through the Holy Spirit: "For as many as are led by the Spirit of God, they are the sons of God. The Spirit itself beareth witness with our spirit, that we are the children of God: And if children, then heirs; heirs of God, and joint-heirs with Christ" (Rom. 8:14,16-17).

We are children of the eternal King living on this side of the veil of death. Like Abraham, neither you nor I have yet fully "received the promises, but having seen them afar off, were persuaded of them, and embraced them, and confessed that [we] were strangers and pilgrims on the earth" (Heb. 11:13). This hope, these promises, are fanned as the coals of a fire, so to speak, by the Holy Spirit. He is at work not only to shape our present lives but also to bring the future glory to the very edge of this present existence.

Images of the Promise

In various ways the New Testament speaks of the glories of the world to come, indicating that we can but "touch the hem of the garment" in this present age. Let us briefly look at three of these images of the promise.

Sealed

Ownership.—The first image is that of the seal. My relatives went to Florida in the early 1820's, while Florida was still a territory. A couple of years ago I did some research on my family and searched among the old legal records of the 1820s and 1830s, stacked like yellowed newspapers in a court house basement. You can imagine my delight when I found, in a weathered old register book of cattle brands, the cattle mark of my great-great-great grandparents, a mark dating from 1825! That mark set apart the Davis cattle and gave protection and recognition to them. The mark, or seal, was very important, and each farmer registered his mark at the court house.

In the New Testament, the seal carries a similar significance. We find the figurative use of seal as a sign of ownership, as a sign of recognition to mark those who belong to Christ, as a sign of membership in the church, as a sign of confirmation of the gifts of the Spirit, as a symbol of power and protection, and as a promise of the glory to come. (See 2 Cor. 1:22; Rom. 8:9; Eph. 1:13-14; 4:30). In the Book of Revelation, we see a beautiful use of the idea in the sealing of God's people with a mark to show they belong to God and will be protected in the coming persecutions (Rev. 1:7-8).

Assurance and power.—The Spirit is given to us as a sign that we belong to God, that we are part of the body of Christ, and that we have been given the power and help of the risen Christ. We have been sealed with the presence of the Spirit as an assurance of our parts in the world to come. As Abraham "received the sign of circumcision, a *seal* of the righteousness of the faith which he had yet being uncircumcised" (Rom. 4:11, author's italics), so have we received the presence of the Holy Spirit of promise as a seal of our salvation and coming glory.

Firstfruits

The second image of the promise is firstfruits. The general Old Testament usage has to do with the first and finest of the field or flock. In the New Testament, Abraham is spoken of as the firstfruits of faith (Rom. 11:16), Epaenetus (16:5) and the house of Stephanas (1 Cor. 16:15) are referred to as the firstfruits of Achaia, and Christ is spoken of as the firstfruits of "them that slept" (1 Cor. 15:20; compare v. 23). The first glorious application of the firstfruits image is to our resurrection. Because Christ was raised from the dead, we have assurance of our resurrection, for Christ is the firstfruits of a mighty resurrection event. As Karl Heim said so powerfully:

> Just as when a dyke in the Low Countries on the shores of the North Sea gives way, even if it is only one little section, we know that, although this is in itself an event of small importance, the consequences are incalculable; beyond the dyke is the tumultuous sea, which will burst through the opening—so Paul knew, when he had met the Risen One, that "He is the first-born of them that slept."[1]

We are told in Romans 8, "ourselves also, which have the firstfruits of the Spirit, even we ourselves groan within" (v. 23). This is the usual idea of firstfruits, and we are assured that the gifts we have received through the Holy Spirit—conversion, sanctification, forgiveness, communion with God, spiritual knowledge, joy, and peace—are but a foretaste, a sample, of the full harvest God has prepared for us in the coming Kingdom. The gifts of the Spirit will be followed by all the glories of sonship!

Guarantee

The third image of promise is guarantee. The idea is similar to that of firstfruits, yet stronger. Several passages speak of the Holy Spirit in our lives as a guarantee or earnest of our inheritance in glory (2 Cor. 1:22; 5:5; Eph. 1:13-14). Christians live in an atmosphere of promise. The guarantee, the *arrabōn*, of this promised glory is the Holy Spirit who is given by the Father as a first installment or down payment on the glory to come. The ancient papyri show many instances of the secular use of the word *arrabōn* in this way.

As a high school boy, I worked in a clothing store and can still see in my mind's eye the gray filing drawer in which we kept the sale tickets for merchandise "laid away" in the back room of the store for customers. Every Saturday a steady stream of people came to pay on their purchases, so they could have them by Christmas or some other special time. If we lift the analogy to a higher level, God has made a down payment, a first installment, toward the full gift of glory for us in sending the Spirit into our lives.

Son and Brothers: Slaves No More

Slaves No More

The New Testament assumes that all of us were slaves before coming to Christ. *Slave* implies a total obedience to the will of someone or something other than ourself. Various passages speak of our slavery to sin (Rom. 6:6-7,12,14,16-23), uncleanness (v. 19), idols (Gal. 4:8-9), spirits of the universe (v. 3), passions and pleasures (Titus 3:3), and to the law (Rom. 7:1).

Jesus said: "No man can serve [as a slave] two masters; for either he will hate the one, and love the other; or else he will hold to the one, and despise the other. Ye cannot serve God and mammon" (Matt. 6:24). In Jesus' time some slaves did belong to *two* masters. In fact, one master could free his portion of a slave while the other master would not, leaving a man half free and have slave![2] The words of Jesus show how absurd it is for people to think they can truly give exclusive and complete commitment to two masters. Sin enslaves us, separates us from God, takes away from us the possibility of deciding the course of our lives, brings forth the rotten fruit of death, and tries to steal the final victory.

Slavery is also seen in a positive way as an image of the Christian life. It is used in connection with our changing masters. Being set free is not the goal of conversion. The contrast is not between being either a slave or a free person, but between being a slave to sin or being a child of God. Freedom from slavery, a freedom we receive only in Christ (Gal. 5:1; 4:3-5), is important because only then are we free to choose whether we wish to follow Christ (Rom. 6:18-23; 8:21 *f.*; Gal. 4:21-31).

Jesus told the disciples, "Henceforth I call you not servants [slaves]; for the servant knoweth not what his Lord doeth: but I have called you friends; for all things that I have heard of my Father I have made known unto you" (John 15:15). Yet verse 14 makes clear that this fellowship as friends is dependent upon our doing what Jesus commanded: "Ye are my friends, if ye do whatsoever I command you." Paul certainly understood that the only way to rise above slavery is to fully commit ourselves to Christ.

Sons and Heirs

Sonship.—The contrasting reality to slavery is sonship, as we see in the words of Jesus: "Verily, verily, I say unto you, whosoever committeth sin is the servant of sin. And the servant abideth not in the house for ever: but the son abideth ever" (John 8:34-35). So the Christian is rescued from slavery into sonship (Gal. 4:5; Rom. 8:15,23).

We realize that our adoption by God is possible because of Jesus' coming as the only begotten Son (Gal. 4:4-5). Our sonship is shaped by His sonship (Rom. 8:29), and we become heirs of God and joint heirs with Jesus.

The Holy Spirit leads us into sonship (Rom. 8:14). Because we are sons, God puts the Spirit into our hearts, crying "Abba [Father]," and leading us to say the same (Gal. 4:6; Rom. 8:15). This is the term Jesus used in prayer to the Father, and it carries a flavor of intimacy and dependency—very much like our saying "Daddy." The Holy Spirit is both the "Spirit of [sonship] (Rom. 8:15) and the "Spirit of his Son" (Gal. 4:6). The Spirit testifies to us that we are children of God by planting that cry of "Father!" in our hearts.

One of the finest descriptions of our sonship is that of McLeod Campbell:

> Let us think of Christ as the Son who reveals the Father, that we may know the Father's heart against which we have sinned, that we may see how sin, in making us godless, has made us orphans, and understand that the grace of God, which is at once the remission of past sin and the gift of eternal life, restores to our orphan spirits their Father and to the Father of spirits His lost children.[3]

Heirs.—Joint heirs with Christ! Covictors with Christ! The relationship of being heirs is brought about and sustained by the Spirit. The writer of Hebrews spoke eloquently of the kinship of Christ with us, His young brothers, saying that Jesus partook of flesh and blood that "through death He might destroy him that had the power of death, that is, the devil; And deliver them who through fear of death were all their lifetime subject to bondage" (Heb. 2:14-15). Jesus is the original, and truly righteous, elder brother!

Our kinship with Christ means we share Christ's ultimate victory. To us as conquerors shall be granted the privilege of sharing His suffering ("joint-heirs with Christ; if so be that we suffer with him, that we may be also glorified together" Rom. 8:17), and of sharing His throne in glory (Rev. 3:21). We are certain of ultimate and final victory because Jesus is victorious: "Be of good cheer; I have overcome the world" (John 16:33). In his First Epistle, John wrote, "Whatsoever is born of God overcometh the world: and this is the victory that overcometh the world, even our faith" (5:4).

Romans 8: To View the Land

The eighth chapter of Romans is the high point of Paul's letter and the glorious mountain peak of his theology. Some scholars feel that in this eighth chapter Paul surveyed all the distance he had covered in the letter—from the dismal darkness of the godless pagan in chapter 1 to exult in the life in the Spirit in chapter 8.

That is probably true, and it may also be true that chapter 8 is artificially divided from chapter 7 (whose dark tones are lightened only by its closing verses) and that the problems of chapter 7 are answered with a glorious certainty as Paul looked on out to the end of time in chapter 8. It is, indeed, a soaring description of spiritual hope, final and victorious. In Romans 8 are three great truths about the promised victory through the Spirit: the promise that we shall be with Him and be like Him, the hope of victory for all of creation, and the tremendous comparison of this world and the next.

With Him and Like Him

The blessed hope toward which the Spirit points us is twofold: to be like Christ and to be with Christ (Rom. 8:23-25,28-30,35-39). Jesus' followers' glorious hope is to be with Him. The finest description of heaven is found in John 14: Jesus declared that He was going to prepare a place for His followers, and would come back to escort us to that world of glory, that where He is, there we may be also! The rewards promised by the Spirit to those who overcome in the seven churches of Revelation are tied to the presence of Christ in glory (Rev. 3:5,12,20-21).

To be like Jesus is the goal of all the spiritual shaping we as Christians undergo by the Spirit. Romans 8:29 tells us that God's intention, God's predestination, is that we be conformed to the image of Jesus. We do not understand all that verse says, but it is clear that our becoming like Jesus is the primary work of the Spirit in our lives (2 Cor. 3:18). We submit to the ministry of the Holy Spirit in our lives and expect to become like Christ on the victorious last day: "Beloved, now are we the sons of God, it doth not yet appear what we shall be: but we know that, when he shall appear, we shall be like him; for we shall see him as he is" (1 John 3:2).

A taste of that life which we will share in Christ's presence and likeness is given us in this world. The character which the presence of the Spirit has put into our lives—joy, peace, hope (Rom. 15:13)—is a firstfruits, a foretaste, a sample of the victory to come beyond this world (Rom. 8:23). The future will be like the joy which we presently experience in our highest, best, and closest moments with the Spirit.

Our hope is not based on what we are presently missing in this world of sin, what we *have not* received, rather on what we *have* received in the Spirit. Since the Holy Spirit dwells in us, we have already moved out of a natural existence, lives moving toward the grave and judgment, and are moving toward lives which are supernatural (Rom. 8:1-2). The early churches had a tradition of serving milk and honey to new converts at their first communion to symbolize the real presence of the world to come. The resurrection has taken place in us: We have passed from death to life.

The New Testament teaches us that the more we sense the nature and reality of the world to come pressing in on this world in our lives, the more we long for the fullness of that glory. So, in terms of Romans 8:22-23, we groan because we sense the coming glory. We are like sick folk on the road to recovery, who fret and chafe under the present restrictions soon to be removed.

The Victory for All Creation

Paul mentioned a marvelous concept in Romans 8:19-22: All creation groans with us, yearning to be set free! The very ground was cursed due to Adam's sin (Gen. 3:17). Mountains, trees, rocks and hills are in a twisted bondage due to the sin of mankind. Paul said they wait in anxious, tiptoe eagerness for the dawning of the glorious freedom of the sons of God! "And I saw a new heaven and a new earth" (Rev. 21:1).

The Glorious Comparison

In Romans 8:18 Paul made a tremendous affirmation about the coming victory and did so with a studied understatement: "I reckon that the sufferings of this present time are not worthy to be compared to the glory that shall be revealed in us." To say "I think," or "I hope," would have been lame and weak in view of all Paul's trials and tribulations and the darksome earthly future which he could no doubt see ahead. "I reckon" has the idea of adding up columns; it is a bookkeeper's term. He had totaled up this world's burdens, struggles, and trials and then compared them with the glorious victory of the kingdom of God even now breaking into our lives through the indwelling presence of the Spirit.

"I reckon that the sufferings of this present time are not worthy to be compared with the glory that shall be revealed in us." The burdens of this world—of this present time—are limited but the coming glory is unlimited! "Eye hath not seen, nor ear heard, neither have entered into the heart of man, the things which God hath prepared for them that love Him" (1 Cor. 2:9).

Notes

1. Karl Heim quoted in James Stewart, *A Faith to Proclaim* (New York: Charles Scribner's Sons, 1953), p. 134.

2. See Karl H. Rengstorf, "doulos," in *Theological Dictionary of the New Testament,* Gerhard Kittel, ed. (Grand Rapids: Wm. B. Eerdmans Publishing Co., 1976), 2:270.

3. McLeod Campbell quoted in James Stewart, *A Man in Christ* (New York: Harper and Brothers, n.d.), p. 254.

Bibliography

Barclay, William. *The Promise of the Spirit*. Philadelphia: Westminster Press, 1960.

Bonner, Gerald. *The Warfare of Christ*. New York: The Faith Press, 1962.

Chafer, Lewis S. *He that Is Spiritual*. Findlay: Dunham Publishing Co., 1918.

Dodd, C. H. *The Epistle of Paul to the Romans*. Glasgow: Fantana Books, 1959.

Dunn, James D. G. *Jesus and the Spirit*. Philadelphia: The Westminster Press, 1975.

Herring, Ralph A. *God Being My Helper*. Nashville: Broadman Press, 1955.

Hinson, E. Glenn. *A Serious Call to a Contemplative Life-Style*. Philadelphia: The Westminster Press, 1974.

Kelly, Thomas R. *A Testament of Devotion*. New York: Harper and Row, 1941.

Küng, Hans. *The Church*. Garden City: Image Books, 1976.

Morgan, G. Campbell. *The Spirit of God*. Westwood: Fleming H. Revell Co., 1953.

Moule, C. F. D. *The Holy Spirit*. London: Mowbray and Co. Ltd., 1978.

Peck, John. *What the Bible Teaches About the Holy Spirit*. Wheaton: Tyndale House Publishers, Inc., 1979.

Robinson, H. Wheeler. *The Christian Experience of the Holy Spirit*. Glasgow: Fantana Books, 1962.

Stagg, Frank. *The Holy Spirit Today*. Nashville: Broadman Press, 1973.

Underhill, Evelyn. *Mystics of the Church*. Cambridge: James Clarke & Co. Ltd., 1975.

Scripture Index

Genesis
3:17 137
5:24 58
Leviticus
11:45 27
Psalms
34:1-7 128
51:11 21
137 119
Joel
2:28-32
Matthew 118
6:6-18 59
6:6 80
6:24 133
7 101
7:15-23 101
10:20 14
12 125
12:22-32 107
12:25-26 126
12:28 126, 130
12:32 108
14:23 59
18:19 116
Mark 118
1:25 35
1:35 59
3:22-30 107
3:28-29 107
5:8,12-13 35
9:19 103
9:29 60
11:23-25 60
13:33 60
Luke 110, 118
2:40 58
4:1-13 59
4:13 123

6:12-13 59
9:23 52
10:18 123
11:1-13 59, 60
11:5-13 100
11:14-20 107
12:12 19, 120
21:12-15 19
22:3 123
22:31-32 60, 123
22:53 123
23:28 123
23:34 60
John 48
1:12 40
1:32 18
1:33 18
3 28
3:3-5,7-8 28
8:34-35 134
11:42 60
14—16 14
14, 14, 135
14:1 14
14:14 15
14:13-14 60
14:16-18, 26 17
14:16 14, 15, 21
14:17 15, 21
14:18 17
14:26 15
15:1-8 101
15:14 134
15:15 134
15:26-27 15
15:26 14, 15, 17
16 14
16:7-8,13 14
16:7,13-15 17

16:7 15
16:8-11 15
16:13 15, 48
16:14 48
16:16 17
16:33 135
17 60, 115
Acts 110
1:5 28
1:8 40, 120
2 31, 111
2:4 f. 49
2:14-36 95
2:16-21 22
2:38-39 21
2:39 21
3 117
4:8 31, 49
4:20 120
4:31 116
4:34-35 114
4:36-37 114
5 52
5:3 114
6:1 98
7:48 41
8:16-18 21
8:26,29,39 120
9:4 19
9:5 19
9:17 21
10:14-19 19
10:19-20 120
10:44-45 21
11:15-18 29
13:2 120
13:8-11 98
15 119
15:8 21

15:28 16, 119
16:6-10 120
16:6 19
16:7 19
20:28 119
22:7 19
22:8 19
26:14 19
26:15 19
Romans 125
1 135
1:24 f. 38
4:8 48
4:11 48
5 48
5:2 42
5:3-5 48
5:7 104
6 51
6:1-13 37
6:1-11 22
6:1-10 51
6:2-4,6,8,11 44
6:2 37
6:3-4 29
6:4 38
6:6-7,12,14,16-23 133
6:6 37
6:11-13 51
6:11 38
6:13 38
6:18-23 133
6:19 38, 133
6:22 36
7 135
7:6 37
7:14-25 35
8 51, 132, 135-137
8:1-13 35
8:1-2 136
8:2 36
8:5-9 36
8:9-11 17, 19
8:9 131
8:10-11 22
8:13 37, 38
8:14, 16-17 130
8:14 134
8:15,23 134
8:15 134
8:17 135
8:18 137
8:19-22 136
8:21 f. 133
8:22-23 136
8:23-25,28-30,35-39 135
8:23 136
8:26-27 116
8:26 42, 61, 84
8:28-31 37

8:29-31 37
8:29 30, 134, 136
9:1-3 61
9:1 61
10:1 61
11:16 132
12:1-2 106
12:6-8 94
14:15-17 113
14:17 36
15:13 136
16:5 132
1 Corinthians 117, 121, 125
1:26-27 40
2:4 40
2:9-10 47
2:9 137
2:14 53
3:1-3 53, 54
3:1 45
3:16-17 111
3:16 41
3:17 41
4:21 121
5:5 126
6:11 32, 38, 39
6:17 17
6:19 41
7:5 127
7:7 94
7:40 49
8 49, 113
8:13 113
11:3-10 96
11:26 118
12—14 93
12 93, 112
12:3 93
12:4-6 17, 95
12:6 99
12:7 91
12:8-10 94
12:9 104
12:12 111
12:13 29, 33, 112
12:28-30 94
12:28 99
13 92, 102
14 91, 94
14:1 129
14:4-5,18,39 96
14:18-19 61
14:19 61
14:32 94, 95
14:33 115
14:34-35 96
14:39 95
15:20 132
15:23 132
16:15 132

2 Corinthians 121, 125
1:22 131, 132
3:17 36, 136
3:18 37
5:5 132
5:14-15 37
5:17 29
6:16-17 41
11:14 129
12 61
12:8-9 82
12:9-10 40
12:21 38
Galatians 51
2:11-12 121
2:13-16 121
2:19 37
2:20 17, 44, 55, 126
3:1-3 54
3:2 22, 23
3:3 33
3:17 29
4:3-5 133
4:3 133
4:4-5 134
4:5 134
4:6 84, 134
4:8-9 133
4:21-31 133
5:1 133
5:13-26 35
5:16 36
5:17 44
5:19-26 53
5:22-23 36, 101
5:24 44
5:25 36, 52, 101
6:14 44
Ephesians 125
1:13-14 131, 132
1:16 61
1:19-20 39
1:22-23 111
2:1-7 37
2:18-22 111
2:18 42
2:19-22 41
2:22 41
3:16 39
3:17-18 73
4 93, 113
4:2 103
4:4-6 114
4:5 29
4:11 94, 95, 99
4:13 113
4:15-16 111
4:19 38
4:22-24 37
4:22 37

139

4:30 105, 106, 131
5:3,5 38
5:8 38
5:18-20 42
5:18 31, 52, 115
5:19 116
5:26 38
6:10-18 128
6:12 124
6:16 128
6:17 48
6:18 84
Philippians 125
1:4 61
1:19 36
2:1-4 114
2:1-2 34
2:12-13 47
3:4-7 23, 45
3:12 23, 45
3:17-19 53
4:7 103
4:13 39, 52
Colossians
1:11 39
1:27 17
2:12 29
2:20 37, 44
3:1-10 37
3:1-5 52
3:1 36, 38
3:3 37, 44
3:5-7 53
3:8-9 37
3:13 103
1 Thessalonians
1:2 61
1:5 49
1:6 103
2:3 38
3:5 127
4:3 28
5:17 86
5:19 105, 106
5:22 129
5:23-24 34
2 Thessalonians
1:9 30
2:13 29
1 Timothy 125
3:7 127
2 Timothy 125
1:3 61
1:7 39
1:14 17
2:3 125
Titus
3:3 133
3:5 17, 38

Hebrews
2:1 45
2:3-4 98
2:14-15 135
3:7 17
4:12 49
4:15 59
5:8 58
6 54
6:3 54
9:8 17
9:14 17
10:15 17
10:22 79
10:23,25 45
11:13 131
James
5:16 84
1 Peter
1:2 17, 32, 33, 38
1:11 17
1:12 49
1:15-16 32
2 112
2:2 45
2:5 111
2:9 30, 112
2:24 44
3:7 79
3:15 iii
3:18 42
3:19 123
5:8-10 123
5:8 129
1 John
1 115
1:3 115
1:6 115
1:7 38, 115
1:9 80
1:19 106
1:20-26 115
3:2 136
3:24 17
4:1-6 17
4:1 129
4:4 126
5:4 135
Jude
20 84
Revelation 50, 121, 128, 131
1:5 38, 39
1:7-8 131
1:10 17, 48
2—3 121
2 50, 121
2:1,7-8,11 17
2:5 45
2:7 50

3 50, 121
3:5,12,20-21 136
3:15-16 45
3:21 135
4:2 17
4:8 86
5 116
12 123
12:11 128
12:12,17 123-124
12:12 124
14:13 17
17:3 17
21:1 137
21:7 130
21:10 17